Waiting in the Wings

Gaye Manwaring

WAITING IN THE WINGS

Letters of a Pilot in World War II

Gaye Manwaring

Waiting in the Wings: Letters of a Pilot in World War II by Gaye Manwaring.

First edition published in Great Britain in 2021 by Extremis Publishing Ltd., Suite 218, Castle House, 1 Baker Street, Stirling, FK8 1AL, United Kingdom.
www.extremispublishing.com

Extremis Publishing is a Private Limited Company registered in Scotland (SC509983) whose Registered Office is Suite 218, Castle House, 1 Baker Street, Stirling, FK8 1AL, United Kingdom.

Copyright © Gaye Manwaring, 2021.

Gaye Manwaring has asserted the moral right under the Copyright, Designs and Patents Act 1988 to be identified as the author of this work.

The views expressed in this work are solely those of the author, and do not necessarily reflect those of the publisher. The publisher hereby disclaims any responsibility for them.

This book is a work of non-fiction. Unless otherwise noted, the author and the publisher make no explicit guarantees as to the accuracy of the information included in this book. All hyperlinks indicated in the text were considered to be live and accurately detailed at time of publication.

This book may include references to organisations, feature films, television programmes, popular songs, musical bands, novels, reference books, and other creative works, the titles of which are trademarks and/or registered trademarks, and which are the intellectual properties of their respective copyright holders.

All rights reserved. No part of this publication may be reproduced, stored in a retrieval system, or transmitted, in any form or by any means, electronic, mechanical, photocopying, recording or otherwise, without the prior permission in writing of the publisher.

This book is sold subject to the condition that it shall not, by way of trade or otherwise, be lent, re-sold or hired out, or otherwise circulated without the publisher's prior consent in any form of binding or cover other than that in which it is published and without a similar condition including this condition being imposed on the subsequent purchaser.

A CIP catalogue record for this book is available from the British Library.

ISBN: 978-1-9996962-7-6

Typeset in Goudy Bookletter 1911, designed by The League of Moveable Type. Printed and bound in Great Britain by IngramSpark, Chapter House, Pitfield, Kiln Farm, Milton Keynes, MK11 3LW, United Kingdom.

Front cover artwork is Copyright © Matt Gibson at Shutterstock.
Frontispiece artwork is Copyright © Matthias G. Ziegler at Shutterstock.
Incidental stock images sourced from Pixabay unless otherwise indicated.
Author photos are Copyright © Pete Glen and Andrew Wilson, all rights reserved.

Cover design and book design is Copyright © Thomas A. Christie.

Internal photographic illustrations are Copyright © Gaye Manwaring and are sourced from the author's personal collection, unless otherwise indicated.

The copyrights of third parties are reserved. All third party imagery is used under the provision of Fair Use for the purposes of commentary and criticism.

The image quality of some of the photographs reproduced in this book reflects the historical nature of the source material.

This book is dedicated to the memory of
my parents

Joan Manwaring
484527:
20 January 1922 – 16 October 2002

Len Manwaring
1334965:
24 July 1921 – 17 May 2017

I was so lucky to have parents who loved each other and me so much.

The proceeds from my royalties from this book will go to the Montrose Air Station Heritage Centre, where there is an exhibition case dedicated to them.

Contents

Historical Context .... Page i
Prologue .... Page 1
Before the War .... Page 5

The Letters
1. Home Guard .... Page 11
2. Called Up .... Page 51
3. South Africa .... Page 91
4. Back in the UK .... Page 153
5. Peacetime .... Page 211

After the War .... Page 239
Acknowledgements .... Page 259
About the Author .... Page 261

Historical Context

FLYING instructors are the unsung heroes of aviation. They pass on the essential skills of flying but at what cost to their mental wellbeing and physical safety?

The story of the Royal Flying Corps/Royal Air Force Montrose through both World Wars is about flying training and we are fortunate in that so many men have left an account of their experiences as both instructors and pupils. There is no better story than that told by Len Manwaring.

Len joined the RAF in 1941 and was selected for flying training and sent to the USA at a time when the Americans were not yet in the war. His experience of the American flying training system must have been a culture shock but he went from there to Canada, home to Britain and then overseas again to South Africa where he completed his training and got his wings. Instead of being posted to an operational squadron he was sent to No2 Flying Instructors School at RAF Montrose; he had been selected to become a flying instructor.

The flying instructors at Montrose were from many parts of the British Empire and beyond but one thing characterised them, they were above average pilots. No2 FIS reserved the best pilots for instructors. The instructors at Montrose often met in the Star Hotel and jokingly expressed their feelings about this by devising a new decoration, the Montrose Star, with a yellow ribbon for avoiding combat with the enemy. Some tried hard to get into combat. "Chile" Cooper (from Chile) eventually got his wish to fly Mosquitoes. He was posted missing after his aircraft disappeared. Mark Foss (from Canada) was never allowed to leave Montrose.

Being an instructor was no easy option nor was it a safe one. Instructors accumulated more flying hours than other pilots and had to be more versatile. Squadron Leader Betty, Chief Flying Instructor, filled six logbooks. Flt Lt Marshall flew seven different aircraft types in one week. Experience did not guarantee survival. Two of the most experienced instructors, Flt Lt Powrie and PO Brown were both killed in a mid-air collision. PO Mark Foss never forgot the time he put a Harvard into a spin at 10,000 feet to demonstrate how to regain control. He eventually levelled out at 200 feet above the runway. Len Manwaring would have known some of these men. The instructors were members of a close-knit elite.

Some aircraft were more popular than others. Len liked the Airspeed Oxford, a twin-engine bomber trainer, adapted from a civilian aircraft, which came into service at Montrose in 1938. It continued in RAF service until the 1960s, long after he had left the service and embarked on a new career.

Service life in the war years involved frequent relocation. Len and his fiancée and later wife, Joan, were both in the forces, which took no account of personal feelings or circumstances when making postings. Like many couples they kept in touch by writing letters but unlike most, their letters have survived. They reveal feelings that are familiar but are set in a time and place in history that gives them a special significance.

Dr Daniel Paton
Montrose Air Station Heritage Centre

Len and Joan, c.1940

Some of the letters and airgraphs

WAITING IN THE WINGS

Gaye Manwaring

Prologue

MY Dad, Len, was a pilot during the Second World War, and married my Mum, Joan, in July 1944. They were happily married for 58 years. When he was 85, a few years after my Mum died, my Dad married Elizabeth. After ten happy years he died in 2017 aged 95. A year later, Elizabeth and I found some photos and RAF memorabilia including his logbooks in his attic in Sussex. I took them to the Montrose Air Station Heritage Centre. They were very pleased to have them, and created a display case to exhibit some of the items.

Another year on and, deeper in his attic, I found a collection of letters written by him to my Mum between 1940 and 1946, when he was demobbed and left the RAF. There are 412 letters, and I have selected around a third of the most interesting ones. These are not all the letters that he sent during this period. Some were never delivered because they were lost at sea. There are very few from my Mum to my Dad, presumably because he would not have been able to carry them with him on his many postings. Some letters may have been lost during nine house moves over the next 70 years.

I debated whether or not I should read such personal items, but I knew they had already been seen by a war-time censor. In my Dad's will, he left me several items including his "unfinished literary works and manuscripts of her choice with permission to have them published if she so wishes." Although the letters were probably not quite what he intended, I think he would have approved. I also feel strongly that the letters were a gift I was meant to find and to share. I have the sensitivity to omit anything too intimate, and the self-control not even to read anything too personal. The conversational tone of the letters means I can almost hear my parents' voices. It helps me with the process of grieving and has awakened many happy and poignant memories, and the occasional guilt trip.

The letters tell the story of a courtship against a backdrop of the war, and also provide an insight into the social history of the time. I have added occasional comments and memories in places. I referred to my Dad's autobiography, entitled *Brylcreem and Black Ties*, to sort out the timeline of events. I also found Len's journal with the letters. It details his life from June 1941 until June 1942, when he set sail for South Africa. It provides a contemporaneous account of that first year, whereas *Brylcreem and Black Ties* was a retrospective written in 1995 and updated in 2005.

My Dad volunteered in the Home Guard in 1940, aged 18, and was called up in 1941. He joined the RAF and was posted to America, Canada and South Africa to learn to fly many different planes. Then he was sent to Montrose to learn how to teach others to fly, and became an instructor pilot in Gloucestershire. He served in the RAF for five years. He flew 8 different aircraft and during that time he was posted to 30 stations, 5 troopships, 3 air forces and 6 countries.

My Mum began training as a nurse in 1940, aged 18, but after about a year she became ill and returned home. She was called up in 1942 and joined the WAAF as a wireless operator, stationed in Gloucestershire. She was discharged in 1945 as she was pregnant with me. I was born in October 1945, a few months after the end of the war.

Writing this in April 2020 during the Coronavirus pandemic, I am struck by the similarities to the wartime experiences. There are shortages, queues, travel restrictions, anxiety, uncertainty and daily lists of deaths. Yet there is also community spirit, selfless work, gutsy resilience and optimism.

Before the War

MY Dad, Len (Leonard Charles George Manwaring), was born at Lydden Farm in Kent. This is a couple of miles outside Margate, and is now home to a camping site for motorhomes and an animal sanctuary. The family moved into town a few years later. Len's father was the office manager for a firm of solicitors and estate agents in Cliftonville, Margate. He saved money by delivering the office mail by hand, riding around on his bike and being allowed to keep the cost of postage. By 1930 he was able to purchase a small semi-detached house at 13 Kent Road, Cliftonville for five hundred pounds.

Len was an only child, but there were numerous aunts and uncles in Kent and London. Len did well at school, won the high jump one year and also received a bee-keeping certificate. He went to Chatham House Grammar School in Ramsgate and played rugby for the school. He played the piano and won several competitions. His first job was in Margate Public Library, and he studied for his professional library exams. He joined the Home Guard in 1940 together with my Mum's younger brother, Jack.

My Mum, Joan (Joan Rosa Wainwright), lived with her mother, her sister Gladys and Jack at number 7 Kent Road. Her brothers, George and Harry, had already been called up, but it must have been a squash when they were all at home.

My Mum's grandfather died young from tuberculosis, and her grandmother and mother were put into the workhouse. I found a letter from my Mum to my cousin recalling what her mother (my grandmother, Nan) said about her own childhood:

> She was very unhappy. She and the other girls had to wash, make their beds, wash and dress all the youngest ones and see to their breakfasts before having their own and going to school. When they came home they had to do more cleaning, then feed and put the youngsters to bed before having their own meal and going to bed themselves. They were slapped for the tiniest misdemeanour.

My grandmother married and lived in Garlinge, a suburb of Margate. She had four children (George, Harry, Gladys and Joan), but then her husband died. She married a widower (Mr Filmer) who lived close by, and they soon had Jack. Joan went to school in Garlinge and passed the entrance exams for the grammar school, but was unable to take up the place because they could not afford the uniform. She was quite ill for many months with spinal trouble and was only able to attend school part time. But there were other problems with her stepfather, as my Mum explained:

> Life was awful living with him and his tempers. We decided as a family that we had to escape his bullying as

soon as Jack was old enough to leave school. Mum rented a house on the other side of Margate and one day when he was at work we hired a cart, loaded up our belongings and moved out. We left him a bed, a chair and table and cooking utensils. I don't know how we managed as the only money coming in was from me, Jack and Harry and we all had poorly paid jobs. George was in the Army and Gladys was ill. But manage we did and we had never been happier. He found out where we had gone and came to the house, calling through the door for us to go back. But we kept quiet and hid and I never met him again.

Joan worked in Margate Public Library from 1939 until 1940, when she left to train as a nurse at Bromley and Orpington. In 1942 she left due to ill health and returned home to live with her mother, Gladys and Jack. Joan and Jack were called up in 1943 but Gladys was too frail. Joan had adopted the name of Filmer from her stepfather, but later gave her maiden name as Wainwright after her real father.

The Letters

Chapter One
Home Guard

"...but I love you so much..."
January 1940 – June 1941

LEN and Joan had known each other for several years and their families lived in the same street, Kent Road in Margate. Len worked in Margate Public Library and studied for his professional library exams. He was in the Home Guard together with Joan's younger brother, Jack. Joan lived with her mother, her sister Gladys and Jack. She worked as a library assistant with Len until she began training as a nurse.

13 Kent Road
Cliftonville
Margate
Kent
9th January 1940

Dear Joan,

Please do not think for one single moment that I have forgotten you. I delayed my letter to you in order to reply to yours. But alas! There was no letter from Joan. In fact I haven't heard from you since last year. I conclude your letter must be lost, unhappily for me.

Home Guard duties proceed as usual. We have been issued with our winter battledress, which is a vast improvement on our previous suit. Also I have my own rifle and "pig-stickers". I am now training to be an Intelligence Officer and find the lectures most interesting and absorbing. Through our instructor I learn that the Invasion Scare is on once more. More I dare not commit to paper. Maybe I can tell you when I see you in a week or two. I can't really make a promise, but when the invasion comes I will do all in my power to see that Gladys and your mother are alright. Jack has told them as long as they stay indoors Jerry will be far too busy looking after himself to worry about civilians.

Dad has just finished his tea and I've promised to wash up. (Yes, I do some housework such as getting meals ready but of course mostly I just help to eat the things.) I called for Jack last night but Henry had come home unexpectedly for 48hrs so Jack did not go to drill. On Wednesday when I went to tea with your mother I gave Gladys and Jack their first piano lesson. I really must finish now as it's 7.40 and I must get into my uniform. So I must come to an abrupt conclusion.

With all best wishes and hopes for your future success.
Yours,
Len

I learned so many things about my parents that I had never known before I found the letters. I thought that my Mum had trained as a nurse after my Dad had joined the RAF, so my understanding of their timeline was back to front. I did not know my Dad had given piano lessons to friends, and my Uncle Henry was always known as Harry after the war.

* * *

Margate
26th January 1940

Dear Joan,
We've had our first fall of snow – last Thursday morning at 1.45am while I was on duty. By 5.0 am when it was time to come home there was a blizzard raging and it was difficult to walk let alone ride a bicycle. I've also seen my first robin this winter. He comes to breakfast in our garden.

I promised you a verse of poetry. Well here it is but I'm afraid it's not as good as I anticipated:

Drifting, drifting, drifting,
Drifting from dawn til dusk.

Sweeping, sweeping, sweeping
Til the fairway's clear at last.
The murder mines are here again
Our sweepers must sweep clean.
Drifting, drifted, driven
By wind and storm, 'tis seen.
But why this subterfuge and shame?
Our foes can't fight in light
But have to use the cunning means
With all their deadly plight.

After Archie left I was Librarian for a week. You'd be surprised the things a Librarian has to do. Wages sheets, order forms, reports, school books to check etc. Now I have to type Mr Clarke's letters and though "I sez it meself", I don't do too badly now.

Mum has just asked me if you received the card she sent from Herne Bay.

Best wishes,
Len

* * *

Birchington Branch Library
Birchington
Kent
12th February 1940

Dear Joan,

How I should love to write "<u>My</u> Dear Joan" but that is not for me. I am still very disappointed. Last night I could not sleep because of you. And when I did sleep you still haunted me in my dreams. But that is not your fault. I do not blame you at all. How could I? Never have you once led me to believe that you had any real affection for me, but you ought to have told me there could never be anything but friendship between us. For months I have told you I love you but always you have refused to believe it. Although we would have been too young to talk of marriage I think I could have made you happy.

Now that I can't have you I love you all the more. Perhaps I shall get over it. Anyway I'm young so I will have a good try. Thank you for your friendship. Don't you think we might go out as friends? I will not annoy you any more at work. If there is any way in which I can help you at any time please ask me. Please destroy this note, then you will have nothing by which to remember me, except the knowledge that I love you (if that means anything to you).

Sincerely yours,
Leonard

Len and Joan both worked for the Public Library in the centre of Margate, but were often moved to different branches for short periods.

* * *

Birchington Branch Library
21st February 1940

My Dear Joan,

Yes, I mean <u>My Dear Joan</u>, for that is how I think of you. Even you cannot stop me from thinking. I hope you will not mind me writing to you. I realise I ought not to. Also I trust you will forgive me writing in pencil. I find myself more able to express my thoughts in pencil and also think it less formal and more friendly.

Please forgive me for pestering you, Joan, but I love you so much that I want to be near you every minute. My dear, please let me be more than a friend. You can't think how much you mean to me. I need you mentally – you act as a stimulant. Desire you physically? Well I don't know about that yet – but I should love to be able to hold you in my arms. You asked me what I saw in you. Well, firstly I see a clean upright truthful young woman. I admire your character, your independence. I like the way you smile, your little hands. I love the many expressions and mannerisms you have.

For months now I have told you I love you, but always you have refused to believe it.

Goodbye My Darling,
Leonard

I had always assumed that my parents had been childhood sweethearts, so it was a shock to realise that my Mum spurned my Dad for so long. He was amazingly persistent, but she did after all keep his letters.

***

Birchington
18th March 1940

Dear Joan,
After our conversation this morning I have been trying to think how I have offended you. The one reason I can think of is this. I have gone back on my word in that I still want to make love to you and put my arms around you. The reason is because you are going out with Sid when you have no more idea of loving him than of flying. You say he regards you merely as a friend so that puts Sid and myself on the same level. If you can honestly tell me you love Sid then I will wish you every happiness, but never doubt my love for you.

I gave you a calendar for the children's library, also lent you my watch. Twice I did the papers for you in the morning. I went to Lanes and got you a catalogue of Nelson's classics to see if there was a Milton amongst. Only yesterday I brought a palm cross back from church for you. Do you think I would have done these things if I didn't love you? I love doing such things for you.

Yours sincerely,
Leonard

* * *

7 Kent Road
Margate
23 March 1940

Dear Len,

I agree about the Armistice, consider it signed, sealed and delivered. I hate staying in bed, because except for a temperature and a continuous "itch" I feel perfectly all right. I suppose you might call this poetic justice after all I said about wanting to have it. About coming to see me again. Yes, do. After all I am, to all intents and purposes, ill and one's <u>friends</u> always visit when one is ill, don't they. Anyway, since when have you been a person who does things that are <u>done</u>. It cheers me up when people come to see how I am anyway. I trust you can read this but it is awkward writing in bed.

    A happy Easter to Mr and Mrs Manwaring and of course to you too.

    Au revoir,
    Joan

Thanks for the card. It was my finest one.

* * *

Margate
20th April 1940

My Darling,

So many things I could write which would all lead to the same thing, that I love you more than anything else in the world. You say it is infatuation, but I just <u>know</u> that I love you. For months now I began to feel different towards you, began to admire you and to like the way in which you did things. I found you to be sensible, so level-headed, so strong in your ideals – in fact so different from the majority of young women I know. But it was not only for these qualities that I began to love you, but for yourself – the <u>real you.</u> I tried not to love you, I think for Shirley's sake, but in January I found it was love I felt for you and not just infatuation.

    One vice I know I have is jealousy. I am jealous that Sid, as only a friend, should be able to go out with you, whereas I cannot. Then there is Shirley. On Tuesday night while I was talking to her an aeroplane passed overhead and she said she wished it would drop a bomb on her. This is rather terrifying. She was very upset. I don't love her anymore than you love me yet she says she loves me. You tell me, at eighteen, that I do not know my own mind. Shirley is only <u>sixteen</u> yet she thinks she knows her own mind. I suppose <u>you</u> know <u>your</u> own mind, at <u>eighteen</u>. Yes of course <u>you</u> do. You do not want love, just friendship. If <u>I</u> don't know my mind, <u>you</u> certainly <u>don't</u> know yours.

    <u>Your own darling,</u>
    <u>Leonard</u>

I was quite surprised to discover that both my parents had had other sweethearts. I had never heard any mention of them, although I found some postcards from Shirley (Shush), clearly a family member, to my Dad's mum. I think she was my Dad's second cousin and they had been very close as children.

* * *

Margate
7th May 1940

Dear Joan,

I want you to know how happy you have made me tonight. Perhaps I shall never feel like this again, yet I will always remember my present happiness and have the knowledge that you once held me in your arms.

Always be as kind, gentle, true, loyal as you are now, and you too will find happiness I'm sure. It is not necessary for me to tell you how much I love you. You will always have a friend in me; one to whom you can come if ever you need help.

If ever you change your mind please remember a silly, sentimental boy. In the meantime I hope you will be happy in your friendship with Sid. I still can't realise that this is the end. Perhaps it isn't! Who knows? Yet I will try to do what you want however hard I may find it.

    Think of me sometimes
    Len

* * *

Westgate-on-Sea Branch library
9th May 1940

Dear Joan,

When I wrote to you on Thursday I thought it was for the last time, but things don't seem to be quite right between us. Please read this before you go to bed. If I have done or said anything which has offended you I am truly sorry. Please tell me why you are so unkind to me and what I have done to deserve your contempt. You don't know how it hurt me to be unkind to you this morning, but I think you asked for it. I now ask for your forgiveness.

If the happenings of Tuesday are worrying you, please don't worry any more. Those things were meant to happen. We were meant for each other. Many things tell me so. No doubt we are now in a time of testing. Tuesday was one day of that test. I cannot believe you were unmoved by what happened. Nothing really happened I know, but it meant a great deal to me. Surely you, too, were happy for a while.

So many things happened that day – little things, yet meaning so much if brought together. I almost believe you love me or at least are very fond of me. You were beginning to care for me on Tuesday. Since then I have done something, I know not what, which has made you so different towards me. You said so many things which all point to the fact that you loved me then. I was so happy to be with you that day. But if you love me, Joan, is that a crime? Is it anything to be ashamed of?

Oh Joan! Why, why, why are we at loggerheads now. I'm not poison am I? You were offhand with me on Wednesday, but I thought that after reading my letter you would at least be friendly and smile again. I am sorry if I have done anything to hurt you. But I can't think what it is. I don't think anyone could help what happened on Tuesday, but if anyone is to blame, I am.

Is it possible for me to see you at all soon? Let us be friends again. Why did you not answer me when I asked if you had enjoyed yourself in Deal? That was unkind of you, Joan. There is a saying: "Never let the sun go down upon thy wrath." That is why I have written to you now so that you may read this before you go to bed. Please forgive me, my dear. Say "Goodnight" to me. I always say "Goodnight Joan".

Goodnight and God Bless you.
Len

* * *

Margate
6th June 1940

Dear Joan,

I dare say this will sound very much like a theorem. <u>Given</u>: My virtues and vices comprising my character. My stated actions and words that I love you. <u>Required to prove</u>: That I do really and truly love you as much as I say I do.

It's a tall order. How can I prove I love you if I can never go out with you or be anything but a friend. I know now that you believe I love you but you think it is just at the moment. It is possible that I shall "get over" my love for you but I don't think so. My love for you is something much deeper and truer. Remember Shakespeare? "Love does not alter when it alteration finds." I shall go on loving you whatever happens. I believe I have now passed the sentimental stage in life although I'm only 18, nearly 19.

Up till now I've mentioned only the love I have for the mental and moral side of your being. I haven't given a great deal of thought to your physical being. Does that disappoint you? Of course I love to put my arm around you and kiss your hair, hands and face. I realise that you have one or two nice curves. I know I should never ask you for anything which you would not give willingly. I love the way you nearly always have a smile, the way you walk and carry yourself. I enjoy watching your many expressions. I don't know how to finish this note. I will just end with a few words.

    I love you my dear.
    Your Leonard

***

Margate
21st June 1940

My Dear,

I'm afraid things are not quite right between us. Whoever is to blame I'm sorry that our friendship should be spoilt by these petty quarrels. Let us be real friends once more and forgive all differences.

I know why I'm unhappy. I love you so much and yet I must be content with friendship and a peculiar friendship at that. You are always in my thoughts. Every night I say Goodnight to you – silly of me isn't it?

I do want to be your friend. The lettuces which I planted for you and which I have watered every day are almost large enough to eat and if we're not friendly I will not be able to give you one or two.

All my love for you,
Len

***

Len wrote a story for Joan in an exercise book. It is about 16,000 words long and tells the tale of David Lockwood, who was a pilot with a girl friend called Anne. He crashed and lost his memory, but after a year eventually recovered and found Anne again. Len and Joan at times "played" these characters, and for several years there are some letters between "David" and "Anne" before they achieved their own happy ever after.

DAVID LOCKWOOD
by
Leonard C. G. Manwaring

TO JOAN
the woman I love

JULY 1940
With pleasant memories

* * *

146 Chadacre Road
Stoneleigh Park
Epsom
Surrey
19th August 1940

Joan Dear,
Yes, it does sound rather nice doesn't it? But I think it had better be Dear Joan.

Jolly old train took 2½ hours to get to Victoria by which time I was not a little hungry. I caught the next rain to Stoneleigh on the way passing the wreckage caused by bombs. Apparently quite a number of time bombs have been dropped in this area and have been going off from time to time.

I must tell you how surprised and pleased they were to see me here. Fussed around me like a prodigal son, especially Shirley, bless her heart. After tea, Shirley and I went for a walk over the hills but not far away. Today I am meeting her from work at Epsom and then going to the pictures.

    Cheerio Joan.
    All the best,
    Len

* * *

Margate
4th December 1940

Dear Joan,

Here is a letter to you in your long exile. There were eventually 31 applicants for the assistant posts of which six had interviews on Monday afternoon. Two of them were successful and commenced work on Tuesday morning. Our new assistants are getting 22/6 per week. Mr Gritten pointed out to the committee that this is hardly fair to me so they will try to increase my salary. I think that was jolly decent of him, don't you? Before the interviews Mr Gritten said to me, "What we want, Manwaring, is another Miss Filmer." And when George came in to say goodbye he said what a wonderful girl you were. You liked the work down here didn't you?

Are you allowed to keep pets at the hospital? Enclosed please find one blue Persian kitten + one red bow. He requires feeding all day long, or else not at all, and please tie his bow carefully each morning.

I am not going to say I hope you are enjoying yourself, not homesick because I realise you must be very unhappy. I hope you will soon shake off those feelings of oppression. Your family I know must be hoping and praying that you will be happy. It may help you to know that someone outside the family circle is also thinking of you and praying for you.

Goodbye and Good Luck,
Len

Joan wished to train as a nurse and was sent to a hospital in Bromley in Kent. She was quite unhappy there, and Len's letters must have helped.

* * *

Margate
5th December 1940

Dear Joan,
Well I was right about our letters crossing for I received one from you today. Ah, how pleased I was to have it. I am trying to write this in the guard room at Drapers Road Block.

Joan, how I miss you. I never thought it possible to feel like this. For four days I couldn't really believe you had gone. When Jack and I bought the cakes at Bowkets on Monday night, quite unthinkingly I said that I would buy a rock cake for Joan. I have gone to work at least three times expecting to see you. Silly of me, isn't it?

How good of you to write to me. I'm sure you must be absolutely worn out after your day's work. You are all aches and pains. I wish I could have my share of them, but maybe I will when I have to join up. My poor, poor Joan. O wish I could do all the washing, cleaning etc. for you. How can my little Jennie be made to do all that work? They might have started you off with something easy. And starting at 5 o'clock on the day of your arrival. That's a dirty trick. Don't give my love to Matron anymore. Well try to like it at Bromley and I know people will like you. It was good of the nurses to help you, but don't get down hearted if you are the lowest of the low, my little Jennie will not stay down there very long. Work hard at your studies but have some amusement.

God bless you,
Len

Len had several nicknames for Joan, including Jennie or Jennie Wren.

* * *

Margate
15th December 1940

Dear Joan,

Things are happening down here. Last Tuesday Hitler planted two bombs in the field at the back of our house, luckily causing no damage except to the field. On Friday night Hitler gave us another early Christmas present in the shape of a land mine. We were roused from our sleep at midnight by the wardens and warned to leave our homes. Fortunately this mine did not explode, the Navy having dismantled it, we are now back home.

Joan, I am now free, for I have sat my exam and can now return all the books to the library and take a rest at least until the results are published. The exam questions were quite moderate. I enclose the papers for you to see.

In my last letter I said I wold write some poetry for you. Well here it is. There are other verses to follow in successive letters.

> *Drifting, drifting, drifting.*
> *Slowly the white flakes fall.*
> *Drifting, drifting, drifting.*
> *Slowly they cover all.*
> *And then the wind begins to blow*
> *Sweeps snow against the walls*
> *Drifting, drifted, driven*

Heaping against the walls.
A sight as this is wonderful,
The pure spotless snow.
As beautiful as that which fell
That Christmas long ago.

I send my greetings with this letter. It will not be a merry Christmas or a happy one, yet we can make it pleasant if we try, and think of those less fortunate than ourselves.
Yours,
Len

Len and Joan's brothers built air raid shelters in their back gardens. Kent Road is about a mile from the coast, and the coast is only about 25 miles from France. I remember playing in the bomb craters as a child as they were in the field behind my grandparents' houses. They were just a playground to me, and I was unaware of any sinister meaning. The bomb holes exposed the underlying chalk, but over the years they became overgrown with vegetation and filled with rubbish. Eventually the field became a housing estate and Jack and his family lived there.

* * *

Margate
18th December 1940

Dear Joan,

Can I break down that invisible yet so often tremendous barrier which surrounds you and say My Dear Joan. As a little Christmas gift I send you a photograph of myself which I hope you think is not too conceited of me. May I send my photograph with love? I also intended to send you some chocolate which I have been collecting for you, but your mother tells me she has sent you some. So I will retain mine as a treat in store for you. The diary is also for you and my warmest greetings for you at Christmastide and a wish that we shall all have a happier time in the near future.

> *I greet you this Yuletide*
> *In the good old fashioned way;*
> *That "Peace and Goodwill" message*
> *Seems out of place today.*
> *But instead I ask you*
> *To bid despair begone*
> *The cloud is slowly lifting*
> *Keep smiling – Carry on.*

Goodbye for the present.
    Sincerely yours,
    Len (and because it's Christmas, may I?) x

Chocolate was a rare treat and Joan cherished the small box of chocolates from her Mum, rationing herself to one a day. She kept them in her bedside locker in the nurses' home. She was upset when she reached the bottom layer to find that half of them had been pilfered. She was saddened not so much by the loss of the sweets but because they had been stolen by colleagues she knew. She still felt the sense of betrayal when she told me about it fifteen years later.

* * *

Margate
26th December 1940

Dear Joan,

I have had several very pleasant surprises recently. Firstly, your Christmas gift. This was most generous of you and I shall treasure it forever. Yet at the same time you are a naughty girl to have sent me something when you are so hard up. I've never seen a comb and nail file combined in that way. Thank you very much.

Margate sees very little of the war. Occasional sirens and every time there's a blue moon we have a bomb dropped on us. So you can see things are very quiet here. Your mother misses you, Jack says nothing and Gladys laughs and talks just as loud as ever. Your mother has kindly invited me to tea and pictures on New Year's Day.

Shirley came down for a few days. I was very pleased to see her and we had a nice chat. We went to Canterbury and spent the day with the verger of Canterbury

Cathedral. He knows the Cathedral and its history inside out and told us many interesting things.

May I congratulate you on your first results? Great work but don't slacken. During your period of work at the library you won the respect and admiration of hundreds of borrowers. So your work here was not in vain, nor will it be in vain at Bromley. The road is long and there is no great prize at the end but you will know that to many you have brought comfort and happiness. Keep on with the great work if that is what you want and treat with disdain, as little Hitlers, all the petty annoyances which come along. If after your probationary period you find you can't go on with it, then give it up. I shall be proud to know you as a fully trained nurse, but I shall never be too proud to be your friend even if you return home in three months' time

It's bed for me now for I have HG duty at 1 am tomorrow.

>Au revoir,
>Len

I had assumed that the Home Guard badges and arm bands that I found in the attic belonged to my grandfather (Nandad), but I now realise they were my Dad's.

* * *

>Bombed Road
>Near Hell's Corner

Boxing Day

Dear Joan,
We hope you have been able to spend a nice Xmas in spite of all things. We had a nice party – all went very well, no trouble from Old Nasty. It is still very foggy and we have had one Alert, but no bombs have been dropped so what do we care. It will not be very long now before we shall have our success then I hope for a real good peace.

The Icecream Italian will go first and then we hope to see a final breaking up.

Wishing you a Happy New Year. Hope on.
Mr and Mrs C Manwaring
Cheerio 26.12.40

My grandfather had beautiful copperplate handwriting, though as a child I sometimes found it hard to decipher. This letter to his son's "friend" shows his affection for her and his sense of fun. I assume that "Old Nasty" refers to Hitler and that "The Icecream Italian" is Mussolini.

* * *

Heavenly Villa
Lockwood
England
1st February 1941

Dear Anne,
It isn't often that you receive a letter from me. The real reason is to ask you to do something for me. You know

Miss Filmer, she's at Bromley Hospital with you, well I did say I would take her to see "The Great Dictator". Unfortunately I am unable to do this. With the enclosed Postal Order will you take her to see the film, only be sure she doesn't know the money comes from me? She will not like it, yet if I were there I should pay for her so I don't see it really matters. Tell her it's your birthday present to her. I do hope you will have a happy time and that Joan will not mind you taking her.

    Your affectionate brother,
    David

This is one of the letters between "David" and "Anne", with the fictitious town of Lockwood referring back to the story of David Lockwood.

* * *

Margate
9th February 1941

Dear Joan,
Is it wrong to be ambitious, 'cos there are several things I'd like to do.

1. I have always longed to have a small steam yacht with a crew of about a dozen. In this I'd see the world. Why a small steam yacht rather than the

comforts of a modern liner I can't imagine, but there it is.
2. I believe I've told you this before. I want £200 by the time I am 24.
3. I want to have an income of £5 per week.
4. I want to succeed in something – even Librarianship.

I know I'll never have a yacht, but I will get my £200 and £5 a week. Now this is a strange ambition. I want to sit in a nice comfortable chair with no light save that coming from the fire. I want you to be with me and I want to listen to a recital of the great masters conducted by Wood. In particular I want to listen to Edward Elgar. Do you like Elgar I wonder?

Your family are all well. Henry wasn't able to "pinch" anything when he went back because Jack hid his hair oil and your Mother locked up her matches and blacking. Sunday is the day we have to stand by for 24 hrs ready for "Action Stations". We're going to be called out but no one knows the exact time yet so we have to stay in all day. "Things" are warming up again, things being the invasion scare. We have to be constantly on the alert now.

We've had three falls of snow this winter and rather dull weather. Now for three days we've had lovely sunny days. It makes me feel so happy. Even I have found my-

self singing. I'm beginning to appreciate these little things in life.
 Yours,
 Len

* * *

Margate
15th February 1941

Dear Joan,
I received your letter and was surprised that you are still undecided about staying on in Bromley. I made discrete inquiries of Mr Clarke. If you came home there is every possibility of you coming back to the library, the salary is £1.2.6 per week plus 6% bonus. I'm not trying to persuade you, just telling you of the possibilities.
 I've never had the pleasure of laying out the dead. I've only seen them when they were all peacefully in bed with just a covering over them. It must be horrible to see someone die for the first time, but we get used to everything in time, don't we. I pray that you will soon be able to decide about your future. Whatever you do I shall always be here to help you.
 Good luck my dear and may God Bless you.
 Len

* * *

Margate
25th February 1941

Dear Joan,

Last Thursday I received your letter and I could scarcely believe my eyes. My first thought was to write and ask if you were ill. Did you mean and believe what you wrote? I suppose you did at the time, but surely if you had thought for a moment you would realise that even I am not quite as rotten as that.

About the money. I realised you would be a little annoyed, but thought you would understand. I couldn't send you a ticket so I did the next best thing. I assure you I sent the money in the same way as I include bits and pieces in my letters because I think you might like them. You speak of charity. If I know you are poor, I also realise you aren't so poor that you can't even afford to go the pictures. I should hate to accept charity myself. I know only too well I'm not all that I could be, but I've not sunk so low as to offer charity to my friends. I understand your feelings about this. You can't forget it I know, but can you shelve it with the other unpleasant memories you have of me?

About coming back to the library – I honestly can't understand your attitude. I never realised you could be so spiteful. You intended to hurt me, didn't you? Well you succeeded. I don't remember telling you how to run your life. I realise that you are quite capable of deciding your own future. In other letters you have thanked me for trying to help you. Now you throw it back in my face. Don't you understand that what I did was only to let you know that if you left Bromley there would be a job here for you instead of nothing. Perhaps I did exceed my boundaries of friendship. I will just say that I asked Gladys first before talking to Mr Clarke.

I notice that you wrote "because we have been friends." Did you intend the past tense? I remember saying that I would always be happy to help you. Surely there's nothing wrong with that.

>Write again soon. Yours as ever,
>Len

Joan had always been poor, but she was proud and fiercely independent. Len was trying to help. He knew she was unhappy nursing and explored the possibility of her return to the library, but Joan saw this as interference.

* * *

>Margate
>17th March 1941

Dear Joan,
Don't think I've forgotten you because I haven't written. I didn't answer your letter immediately because if I had, it would have caused another misunderstanding. I really intended not to mention our quarrel. I wish (I hope as

you do) that we had never written those letters. I will forget it. I do hope you will in time. Please tell me all that happened to you as you used to do.

I really am gadding about these days. I went to Canterbury again Saturday evening to a dance. The last time I went dancing was when I went with you and Gladys. I do hope that when you come home we shall be able to go to a dance or a show. Would you like to. We are on duty tonight early so I shall go down to call for Jack about 8.0pm.

>Au revoir,
>Len

* * *

>Margate
>26th March 1941

Dear Joan,

Spring, the sweet spring, is the year's pleasant king. Then blooms each thing, then maids dance in a ring. Cold doth not sting, the pretty birds do sing – cuckoo, jug-jug, pu-we, to-witta-woo. Now ain't that jus' nice an' poetic like. I always remember that because I had to learn it as an imposition at school. It would be so pleasant to go for a walk or ride into the country this season for now the violets are in bloom and soon the primroses and bluebells will be out.

You immoral young woman, picturing me asleep in bed. Oh! Mother will be shocked. Do you know I usually curl up into a little ball. One blessing however – I don't snore. No wonder you can't concentrate on your studies if you allow your thoughts to wander to young men in bed.

Your Mother tells me you have been chosen to go to Orpington. I suppose it was a case of volunteers – you, you and you. Will you be able to have your holiday? Oh! How much I hope you will. Would you like to come to Canterbury with me for a weekend? Catch the bus from Margate and be in Canterbury in time for a dance on Saturday evening. The Cathedral on Sunday morning and the other old places in the afternoon.

    Good night my dear,
    Len

*　*　*

Margate
19th June 1941

Dear Joan,
I have just returned from night school and would like a few minutes with my friend. How are you? Are your poor hands all rough and hard again? I feel so sorry for you and yet so powerless to help. You say you are gloomy – why not read Marcus Aurelius. I've joined the

ATC to help me with Maths, Morse, Navigation etc. and this takes up three nights a week.

I didn't enjoy my holiday as Shirley and I just got on each other's nerves. I tried all I could to please her but we seem to be drifting apart. Our tastes haven't been alike in many things but now even the affection we have for each other doesn't seem to help at all.

Have you heard this before?

Death is a heartache no one can heal.
Memories are keepsakes no one can steal.

Pilots are being trained in the USA. If I go there I shall not be able to get you three yards of silk. So what can I send you from the States? I'm just about to sit down to supper. A special treat tonight – tomatoes, lettuce and cheese. Coo, it ain't arf nice.

Good night dear Joan.

    Yours,

    Len

Throughout my childhood, if anyone was feeling sad or worried we would open the Marcus Aurelius book at random and read the words which somehow always seemed applicable.

* * *

Margate
30th June 1941

My Dearest Friend,

At last I've been called up and though it's about a month too soon I'm eagerly awaiting my trial. Mum is bearing up fine. What a wonderful woman she is! All mothers are, aren't they? I have to report at Torquay by 6.0 pm on Saturday July 5th. Couldn't have chosen a better spot could I, though of course I may only be there a few days. However I'll write to you and let you know what's happening.

I can realise now how busy you were in your last days at Margate. There's a hundred-and-one things to do. Shirley may come down one evening if she can leave work early.

So for the time being Joan, au revoir.

Yours, Len

Len's Mum's first husband was killed in World War 1 after a very short marriage. Then she married Charles Manwaring, Len's father. Len did not know she had been married before until he found the relevant documents after her death. I do not think it was a secret, just something that was not talked about.

* * *

<u>To Jenny</u>
Once upon a time in the country of Cantium there lived a beautiful girl whose name was Naoj. She was very hap-

py living with her mother and father and brothers and sisters.

But one day a sad thing happened. Naoj's father died and she became very sad. She and her brothers were too young to go to work and they became very poor, till at last poor Naoj's mother married another man to give her children food and shelter.

Their new daddy was not a nice kind one like their first daddy had been. He used to beat the children and make poor Naoj's mother cry so much that she took her children away from the bad man and went to live in a different part of the country. Here Naoj and her brothers and sisters soon found work and they settled in their new home and were quite happy once more.

Except Naoj. At times she would be happy, but she could not forget the harsh words of her stepfather and as time went on and she grew up into a young woman she made a vow never to marry anyone (because she didn't want to be unhappy as her mother had been). So Naoj grew up, always helping other people, always telling the truth whatever happened.

Soon after she went to work in a different part of the town and there she met a young man – an ugly young man, but he had a heart of gold. Now this young man's name was Leo and as soon as he saw Naoj he fell in love with her. But he knew she would not even look at him because he was so ugly. Yet one day he did speak to her and Naoj smiled back at him. From then onwards they became friends. At last Leo told Naoj how much he loved her and asked her to marry him. But Naoj told him of her life and how much she had suffered. Upon hearing this Leo was very sad and became more determined than ever to marry Naoj and make her happy. But still Naoj refused and poor Leo worried so much about her that he became very ill.

One day Naoj went to see Leo when he was ill, but when Leo asked her to kiss him she refused. For she knew deep down in her heart that she loved Leo, but if she kissed him she would tell him so, and this she did not want to do because she had made a promise never to marry anyone.

But one day when she went to see him, Leo was so unhappy that Naoj decided to break her promise and marry Leo if he asked her again, for thought she, if I marry Leo it will make him happy and I shall be no worse. Also thought Naoj, Leo might make me happy too. So when the time came for her to leave Leo and he asked her to kiss him "Goodbye" she did so.

No sooner had she kissed him than he changed from being ugly into a very handsome young man. Now Naoj knew for certain that she loved him and said she would marry him. But Leo thought she only said that because he was no longer ugly. At this Naoj was very sad. Then she told Leo why she had said she would marry him, and because he knew that Naoj always told the truth, Leo believed her.

Soon after this they were married and were very happy and when their children grew up Naoj told them they must always tell the truth, always help other people and then they would always be happy.

This "fairy tale" was with the letters from 1940. It is written in pencil and addressed to Jenny, which was one of Len's nicknames for Joan. It is hard to ignore the parallels with Joan and Len's own story. Naoj represents Joan; Leo represents Len. Joan did have a cruel stepfather and her mother did take the children away as soon as they were old enough to go to work. One day while he was out, they loaded up all their belongings and moved to another part of the town where they were poor but happy. Joan did say that she would never fall in love or marry. I am so glad Len persuaded her to change her mind.

Len in the Home Guard

Len and Joan's brother George digging air raid shelter

Bomb holes

Joan and Gladys, c.1940

Joan's three brothers – Jack, Henry (Harry) and George –
in uniform

Joan in nurse's uniform

Chapter Two

Called Up

"...apprehension, excitement, fear..."
July 1941 – June 1942

LEN was called up and did initial training for the RAF in Devon and Cornwall before being sent across the Atlantic for training as a pilot. On his return to UK, he was stationed at various camps in the North. Joan continued as a nurse in Kent before she became ill and had to return home. She was called up and trained as a WAAF in Gloucestershire.

No 1334965
AC2 Manwaring, L.C.G.
Flight 9, 47 Intake
Sefton Hotel
RAF

>Babbacombe
>Devon
>7th July 1941

Dear Joan,

I have now been here two days but it seems like a fortnight for the amount of things I have done is totally amazing. One thing I'm grateful for is that the food is excellent. Bacon for breakfast, a hot meal for dinner, lettuce and pressed beef or sardines for tea and meat for supper. Plenty of bread and butter and cakes and a choice of tea, coffee or cocoa. What more could one ask for?

This preliminary course is being accelerated and we shall only be here a few days. We're not even having time off after being inoculated this afternoon. The amount of kit is staggering and there is more to come. We've had parades and lectures all day today and yesterday, Sunday. I shall be posted at the end of the week to the Initial Training Wing.

Yours,
Len

Butter was a luxury, but one we nearly always enjoyed as a family even soon after the war. Margarine, the butter substitute, came in hard blocks and tasted horrible, quite unlike the tubs of vegetable margarine we have today. Butter was also hard, and we would place the butter dish in front of the fire to soften its contents. This had its problems. Sometimes we forgot about it until it had melted into a pool of ghee, sometimes the fire sprayed it with soot, and sometimes the cat tried to lick it!

* * *

"C" Flight, No 1 Squadron
8 ITW
Highbury Hotel
RAF Newquay
Cornwall
17th July 1941

Dear Joan,

The above is now my resting place for the next 6 or 8 weeks. And what a hectic time we are going to have. Up by 6.15. Breakfast at 7.0. Parade at 7.50 and all rooms to be clean by that time. From 8 until 6pm with ¾ hr for lunch we are hard at work. Morse, Recognition, Maths, Anti Gas, P.T., Drill, Law, C.O.'s lectures and what not. We have navigation in a fortnight's time. We have tea at 6.0 and then the remainder of the evening is our own, but I prefer to take my books out and sit on the sea front and do my studies there where I have the benefit of this fine bracing air and if I tire I can admire the beauty of the Cornish coast.

If there ever was a wild looking place, that region is Cornwall. The sea has cut great bays and inlets into the cliffs and left countless islands. We went down to the sands yesterday for P.T. There are 179 steps. The only inducement to ascend was that tea was awaiting us at the top.

Don't laugh Joan but can you imagine me liking anyone with ginger hair, well Victor Avery has and I do like him. He's 6 ft tall and is someone after my own heart – full of devilment. We both play tennis, dance and what is more important he can understand the earth and its life. He used to work in a bank and apparently had a great time with the girls. But I think girls are out of the picture for us until we've finished our Initial Training Wing.

The food here is still good. We've had salads, fish, cheese, onions, date pudding, roast beef and baked potatoes, in fact everything except ice cream; but I had one in the town so I haven't missed a thing. I'm going to shoot clay pigeons this afternoon and this will be the first time I've aimed at a moving target so here's hoping.

Yours, Len

Len, in typical librarian fashion, decided to document his experiences. He used an old school notebook (labelled "Homework February 1933") and filled it with postcards of the places he visited. There are a dozen colour postcards of Babbacombe and Newquay, as well as about forty of USA and Canada.

* * *

Newquay
3rd August 1941

Dear Joan,
They said "Join the Navy and see the world". But "Join the RAF and see everything," I say. When I leave here I may go abroad and I'll remember to send you three and a half yards of silk. The Red Tape here is pretty thick as is the case I suppose with most training centres. We are not allowed to discuss the work nor the length of the course. Nor can we mention air raid warnings or enemy action. The main thing is that I'm still alive and feeling very fit.

I've passed my Anti-Gas exam with 70%. That's one of the perishers out of the way. Instead of doing P.T. yesterday I did some fencing and quite enjoyed myself. You know – the "Prisoner of Zenda" or "Three Musketeers" stuff. During lectures I usually take notes down in a rough book and copy them into a fair book during my leisure moments (can you hear the sarcasm there?). In this way I find I learn them as I rewrite them. We've started Navigation now and it is the most interesting subject so far. At times however we all wish we'd joined the WAAFs. I've just returned from Church Parade and am sitting on the cliff top where there is a terrific wind blowing all the cobwebs away. I often wish you were down here. How you would enjoy it!

Note that I am a Leading Aircraftsman. I intended to send you a lucky Cornish pixie, but decided you would probably like a reproduction of a Cornish pitcher for it comes with a "good luck" wish from me and you'll be able to put some flowers in it. My uniform does suit me I fancy and we've been issued with a white flash to place in our caps. Oh boy do we look swell. Thank you so much for your letters. You are often in my thoughts and always in my prayers.

    Yours,
    Len

* * *

August 1941

Dear Joan,

I left Newquay on Wednesday morning 21st August at 6.30am and arrived at Wilmslow at about 7.30pm. We were issued with a further uniform to wear in America – khaki twill with red eagles on it. We also have civilian suits, shoes, shirts – in fact a completely new outfit plus a suitcase. We were at this depot nearly a week (much longer than we had expected). We were told definitely there was no hope of leave. So once more at the dead of night we marched down to the station carrying suitcase, kitbag and full pack. My! What a journey – we had to stop almost every two hundred yards. And so on the train to port where we went on board ship about 11 o'clock the following morning (25/8/41).

To cut a long, long story very short we sailed the next day for about 8hrs then dropped anchor. After about two days we once more attempted to get out. This happened three times in all and the rumours that were put forward as to its cause were astounding. On Sunday 7/9/41 after being on board for two weeks we learned that we were to have home leave. On Monday we came into port, left by train for another depot and I was home by 10.0 Wednesday morning. I called to see your Mother and then went to my own home only to find that Mum and Dad were in London. So to London I went on Thursday, but on Friday I had a telegram "Imperative you return to unit at once", so back I had to go. But I'm glad I was able to see Mum and Dad before leaving England.

This time we were on board and sailing within 48hrs of leaving our depot. We are now well out in the Atlantic. It's great and we have one class each day on navigation, aircraft recognition, Morse. By the way, we also help to spot any Jerry planes which may come. I've just finished eating peaches – they were delicious. When I come back I intend to bring a kit bag full of good things. I'll say cheerio now and continue when we get to the other side.

Excerpt from his journal
Oh when on earth will we leave this wretched place – we've been here twelve days. Wonder of wonders we've "set sail" now. Friday Sept 5th too but does it matter? What are my thoughts now? Certainly with the prospect that we are at last underway I'm more cheerful now as is everyone else. (I must say I never was really down in the mouth.) I often think of the folks at home, how they must be wondering! And Shush – I try to hate her and believe the worst of her, but in my heart I know I love her just the same.

* * *

September 1941

Dear Joan,
We are now on board ship we are having excellent food though we're rather cramped. I find a hammock very comfortable. We've had beef, lamb, veal, pork and chicken since we've been here. And that's not all, for we can have as much chocolate, sweets, oranges, apples, cigarettes (6d for 20) that we like to buy. But there's little to do now except eat, sleep and think. We no longer have to carry gas masks with us, but of course they've found another worry for us in the shape of a life jacket.

I often think of you, but last night I wanted to talk to you as I used to. Do you know I really only knew you, the real wonderful Joan, for about five or six months. Quite suddenly I realise we've been at war nearly two years. How much have I changed during that period I wonder. I still feel the same youngish boy that you knew in September 1939, but no doubt other people will find a change in me. I've always loved my home but now it seems that I haven't appreciated it half as much as I ought to have done.

For the time being, goodbye dear friend and may God Bless you and keep you safe. I know you will work hard and at times be depressed. At such times I find it good to think of someone less fortunate than myself and to pray to God.

Yours,
Len

Len also pasted a few other items into his school book along with the postcards. They include documents from the troopship such as a Berthing Card (Third Class) and a Messing Card (No 3 Dining Saloon. "D" Deck Forward. Second Sitting).

* * *

Toronto
Canada
28th September 1941

Well Joan, here I am at last and I'll tell you what I've done. Voyage uneventful – train journey to this depot lasted 36hrs – very welcome – food in abundance and quality is that of a first rate restaurant. Went down the town yesterday – my, the lights!

I'll say au revoir. Good luck in your exams. I hope you are happy.
Yours,
Len

The stay in Canada was a very short one *en route* to the USA. Also in his school book, Len had stuck his non-immigration visa for entry into the United States. It is dated 27th September 1941 and signed by a Vice-Consul. With it is his Alien Registration Receipt Card bearing the fingerprint from his right index finger. There is also a booklet issued to all servicemen about how to behave in America. It forbids press interviews, cautions against expressing opinions about military or political matters, but also talks about the unbounded hospitality the guests can expect. It ends with these words:

> Here is a mutual opportunity to serve the best in both nations by personal contact and understanding. The responsibility is great. It is an individual responsibility. To a very large extent it becomes your responsibility, as well as your privilege.

* * *

Flying Cadets
Air Corp Training Detachment
Camden, South Carolina
USA
8th October 1941

Dear Joan,

At last I am at my Elementary Flying School. On a good map you can just find Camden, a city of 5000 inhabitants, mostly [of African-American heritage]. The white population have given us a wonderful welcome. They took us to the airport in their private cars and on Sunday three fellows and I were invited by a Mr and Mrs Neil to lunch and tea at their country house. It's very hot here. We only wear overalls even when flying.

Quarters here are very good. We have 20 beds in this room. We each have a locker the size of a wardrobe with combination lock and also a table complete with table lamp and ash tray. Food is likewise excellent, though some dishes are strange mixtures. We have table cloths, napkins and [African-American] waiters. Quite gentlemen aren't we?

I went "up" for the first time yesterday and found it surprisingly easy to handle. There is absolutely no feeling of motion while flying straight and level, and turns and banks are quite thrilling.

Good luck Joan.
Yours, Len

In 1941 all flying training was transferred, mainly to Canada and South Africa. These countries were away from the theatre of war and had better weather than the UK. Len's flying training actually began in the United States of America with the US Army Air Force. This was before the US came into the war and in flagrant breach of neutrality laws. Len posted a group photo to his mother showing ranks of RAF and USAF together. It is now displayed in the Montrose Air Station Heritage Centre.

* * *

Camden
20th October 1941

Dear Joan,

At the moment I should be swotting ignition systems on aeroplanes, but it's boring. I am settled down here at last. It's quite a nice place and the people are the nicest I've met, so willing to give us a good time, but this week I've been rather homesick longing to see those who are dear to me, my parents and friends. I guess that's why I'm writing to you now instead of on Saturday.

Last Sunday we were all invited to a polo match and a dinner afterward. Then I and three other fellows were invited on a drive by an elderly couple who showed us the sites of battles in the American Civil War and the War of Independence. Some of the houses built at the times of the Wars are still standing.

Next weekend we have been invited by the Governor of Columbia to dinner. There is also a State Fair there next week. We do appreciate these weekends after being in camp all week. You remember how petty and unnecessary some of the things seemed when you were first at Bromley. Well we are experiencing something similar. The Americans have to be treated like children and consequently we are likewise as we are training with them. One of my friends, quite in fun, saluted another fellow. He got 6 demerits and an hour's punishment tour for that. In case I have given you the wrong impression, I like the individual Americans and I like the country but I'd love to be back in England.

Au revoir, dear, dear Joan. May God keep you safe and well.

Yours, Len

From *Brylcreem and Black Ties*

Possibly the most humiliating aspect of the American way of life was the square meal imposed for alleged insubordination. Instead of eating a meal in the normal way the unfortunate man had to raise each mouthful in a square fashion, the hand going in a right angle from plate to mouth and back again. We British could not get to grips with the psychology behind this form of punishment. Fortunately while I was at Camden none of the British cadets had to suffer this degrading spectacle.

* * *

Camden
5th November 1941

Dear Joan,

With this Christmas greeting I enclose a short letter to tell you the latest news. Last week was a period of events, happy ones and tragic, laughable and serious. On Monday one of the cadets – an American – was up solo and got lost. Eventually he was found and brought home. He had made a forced landing and got stuck in mud. On Tuesday a British cadet turned a plane completely over on its back. On this day another fellow flew into telephone cables and Camden was without telephones for a few hours. Wednesday was the tragedy. Two planes collided while taking off, one got clear but the other crashed and burst into flames. The pilot, a British cadet, was badly burned and had several other injuries. He died the following day. What a terrible blow to his parents in England! His funeral was on Saturday – a full military funeral and we were allowed to wear full RAF uniform. It was a magnificent ceremony. Now he rests beneath the trees and in the ground hallowed by the fallen heroes of the Civil and Independence Wars.

On Thursday I flew solo after 10½ hrs. Usual times are anything from 8-12 hours for soloing. It's a great moment when the instructor gets out and says "It's all yours." A feeling of apprehension, excitement, fear perhaps! I am now an Upperclassman. This constitutes certain privileges not given to the lowerclass, such as leaving barracks on Wednesday and Friday evenings.

Oh dear Joan, I've just had an Army Air Corps check ride and failed. This means that I shall have to go back to Canada. Ten of us failed. It seems such a pity to come all these miles just to fail, but I shall try to remuster as Observer or Air Gunner. Thank goodness two of my closest friends are going to Canada as well. I feel a little disappointed but mainly I think I'm glad to be going back. I have yet to tell Mum that I've failed here. They tell us not to worry, there is no disgrace in failing just bad luck, but that doesn't repair the damage.

I'll write again when I get to Canada. I hope you are keeping well and happy and still doing well in your exams.

Cheerio,
Len

Excerpt from his journal

On Wednesday 29th October, Jack Pritchard was badly burned and injured in his plane. Thursday he died. We went to the pictures, having been given "open post" privilege on account of the accident (to take our minds off it). On Thursday 30th Oct I flew solo after 10½ hrs. My flying is rather erratic and inconsistent. On Friday I "ground looped".

***

RAF Personnel Transit Centre
31 Personnel Transit Unit
Moncton
New Brunswick
Canada
1st December 1941

Dear Joan,

My exploits since writing to you last have consisted mainly of railway journeys. It seems disgraceful that I and hundreds of others are now just wasting our time over here while people at home are not having such a cosy time.

During the journey we had five hours in New York. This is a wonderful city of beautiful things. We saw the Stock Exchange, Empire State Building, Radio City, China Town, the Bowery, oh and heaps of other places. We had been at Moncton about four days when we had to go to Trenton, about 1000 miles west, to go before the Selection Board. I remustered as an observer and right now I am just waiting for a new course to commence. On the return journey from Trenton we had two hours in Montreal. This is the second largest French city in the world. All the shops are dressed for Christmas and they make a wonderful show.

I have bought postcards or souvenirs of each pace I have visited. They ought to make quite an interesting collection. I have some cotton for you which I picked at Camden. It's just a little round ball on the end of a twig. I should like to send you some silk stockings for Christmas but I remember that dear little Jenny is somewhat independent. Would you mind if I sent you some. The element of surprise is of course now gone. Perhaps it would be just as well if you told me the colour and size you would like. I believe stockings are rather hard to obtain in England. I think you will have to pay a duty of sixpence a pair.

Winter has come now in real earnest. We are told there will be eight feet of snow before long. I intend to learn to skate for I expect to be here for about three months. Oh it's a great county, but I'd sooner be doing something useful. I'm quite happy now though, which I wasn't down in America.

I'll say au revoir now with the promise to write again very soon.

    Yours,
    Len

Excerpt from his journal

Went on board *Letitia* and left Halifax at 9.10pm on Monday 15th December. Arrived at Liverpool 3.30pm Thursday 25th December, but the voyage was really bad. On the second day out we ran into a battle, out of that into a storm which lasted two days. The ship was tossed about just like a cork. One of the ships in the convoy was damaged and had to return to port. One day our galley was wrecked temporarily. Then we had to circle around one day because of submarines and mines – narrowly missed a torpedo. Out of that into another storm. Had to wait two days for a British escort. Eventually arrived at Liverpool on Christmas Day.

* * *

C/O Mrs Howard
37 Sea Road
Boscombe
Hants
2nd January 1942

Dear Joan,

Mum wrote to me that you were in Margate. I expect to have leave in a few days' time. Wouldn't it be nice if you were still at home! I think so. Just now I'm fed up – really fed up for the first time. There is absolutely nothing for us to do here. Nobody knows who we are – in fact we should still be in Canada. Most of my kit is lost – we haven't been paid for three weeks and now we don't really know if we can get leave. I'm not complaining. I'm just showing you in what a mess things are down here.

We are in a private house and are very comfortable. We were led to believe that England was starving, but honestly we have far better food here, and more of it, than I've ever had before. I really don't know how the lady of the house manages to give us such wonderful meals. She has three sons in the RAF so we can rest assured she will do all in her power to make us comfortable. There's plenty of life in Boscombe and even more in Bournemouth. Numerous cinemas, concert halls and theatres. Last Sunday I went to the Pavilion to a Symphony concert – one of the pleasures I love most.

At least I can now boast that I had Christmas Day at sea. We had one Christmas dinner the day before because we expected to be travelling in a train on Christmas Day. But we were delayed due to the conditions of war. What a voyage. One day we saw porpoises playing about in front of the ship. So far I've travelled about 15,000 miles – not bad for a little one, is it? From the dust and heat of Camden to the snow of Canada. From there to the cold Atlantic and then down here where it is very mild spring weather.

Au revoir now, but I hope to see you soon.

As ever

Len

Excerpt from his journal
We were posted to Regents Pk London on Sat 7th March. Went to Auntie Dolly's in the evening. While at

London I had a full medical examination including night vision test and X-ray, also intelligence test and finally went before a selection board. Everything was Ok and I was remustered as a pilot.

* * *

9 E.F.TS.
Ansty
Coventry
Warwick
2nd April 1942

My Dear Joan,

This station is about 7 or 8 miles from Coventry and there is no bus or train service. The camp is quite small and very primitive. We are billeted in Nissen huts and have to plough our way across mud and slush to wash or use the latrines – and when we get to the main buildings there are only five wash basins and four lavatories for 80 of us. Last night it was so very cold that I intend to sleep in my inner flying suit tonight.

We expect to be here for 17 days with an intensive course. We fly in the morning and in the afternoon have ground study. The following day we fly in the afternoon with ground study in the morning. The planes here are very frail compared with the Stearmans of the US Army

Air Corps. We'd only been here ten minutes and two crashes had occurred. Oh boy, what a life.

Yes Joan, I agree with you about your views with regard to Good Friday and the Church. But by fighting our war we are also fighting God's war against evil and I don't think it matters whether we fight on Good Friday or not. I do believe in God yet I don't agree with the attitudes of the Church. Many people say there can be no God because of the terrible things occurring in this world. They don't realise that <u>people</u> make these things and that God will not necessarily stop them.

Maybe we can go out once or twice when I get leave. Good night. God bless.

Yours as always,
Len

Excerpt from his journal

Ansty, near Coventry. Arrived here 1st April originally for a 17 day grading course. This was gradually extended until it was 5th May before I went home for 7 days leave. What a change it was for me to have English Officers etc. to train under. I really feel confident of myself in the plane now whereas I didn't in America. During my stay at Ansty I visited Birmingham and Leicester on my days out and once I went to Bath to see Pauline. She is rather unusual and I find it difficult to find my true feelings for her. I think they are of friendship for I didn't think I could really love her as I do Joan. It's strange too about

Joan for she thinks I've changed and I think she has. But on my leave this time we saw quite a lot of each other. Shush by the way is much nicer now, maybe because she is engaged.

*** * * ***

Coventry
22nd April 1942

My Dear Joan,
I'm afraid my leave has been cancelled once more and it will be next Wednesday before I can come home. How glad I shall be to see Margate once again. How happy too, I shall be to see you. Joan, don't think me too sentimental when I say I don't know what I'd do if I didn't have you write to and think of.

I've now been here three weeks. I don't know what I'm going to do till next Wednesday for I have passed my flying test and flown solo. I suppose I shall just go back to my old job of hanging around. I must tell you more about my first solo. I caused quite a sensation among the instructors and pupils and made a perfect landing.

We have two tennis courts in this camp and last night I was fortunate enough to have a game. It's surprising how tired one gets with flying. How the instructors stick it I don't know. Gosh! I feel tired but somehow very happy when I've done my day's work. The unpleasant surroundings and food just don't seem to count. I just pass them over. Can you understand that?

For the time being it's au revoir now.

Yours with love,

Len

Len had no idea then that he would become an instructor. But he was right that it is an arduous and stressful role. Quite a lot of instructors were killed, so it was by no means a safe option.

* * *

Coventry
29th April 1942

My Dear Joan,
At the moment I'm supposed to be having a Navigation lecture, but as usual the officer hasn't arrived. It's tragic the way this camp is run. I told you it is run by civilians. They must have tons of sugar and tea and other foodstuffs stored somewhere, all of which has been pinched from us and those here before us.

In the past three days the weather has been too bad for flying, but its glorious now so I'm hoping for a trip this afternoon or even two trips. Before we leave this school we have to do all the exercises in the air. So far I've done ten, which is about half. Then I have seven days leave, during which time you will be in Canterbury.

I can meet you one night, go to the pictures or a dance and then catch the last bus back to Margate. What do you think of the idea?

Paddy and I went into Coventry on our last day off to see "Ladies Without" at the Hippodrome. It was a revue and very good indeed. We had a lovely ride in – on a donkey cart as far as Walsgrave. Can you imagine me on a donkey cart. As we left camp, the civilians were also leaving in their cars, but would they give us a lift. "No sir, can't stop for mere Air Force boys." They are a rotten lot at this camp.

<u>2 hours later</u>

Here we are again down on the good old "terra firma". Your darling little Lennie has had quite a good trip. I did landings and take-offs and circuits (commonly known as circuits and bumps). Actually I did bump twice, but that's a mere detail.

In your last letter you asked me to think of you sometimes. My dear, you are often in my thoughts and always in my prayers.

 Ever yours,
 Len

* * *

Coventry
29th April 1942

My Dear Joan,

Last Sunday my Flight Commander asked me to show some ATC boys the controls of the plane and how it flies. I was surprised that I knew as much as I did and was able to answer their questions. In the afternoon I was on the shooting range. I'm afraid my score was not very good, but the instructor was quite pleased that I hit the target at all. It's surprising how different a revolver is from a rifle.

On Monday morning I managed to get hold of a plane which nobody needed and had a short trip all by myself. Aren't I a clever boy? Joking apart, it really does feel good to be up there alone. Organised games were arranged later and I managed to get a game of tennis for about 1½ hours.

I have some suggestions about what we can do on our days together. We can start out in the morning and walk to Cliffs End. There we can have lunch, picnic fashion. Then we can visit the old Roman fortress Rutupiai. In the evening we can go to a show. If you would rather ride I daresay I can borrow a cycle.

Did I tell you we've had two very good ENSA shows at camp recently. The last one was worth paying 2/6 to see it. Of course _we_ didn't have to pay but it would have been well worth the money. Roll on Friday – it's pay day. While on this course we are paid 2/- a day danger money while flying. That would be a nice little packet of cash, but the annoying part is we have to pay 6/6 a week income tax.

*　*　*

Margate
12th May 1942

Joan, my darling,

At last I have thought of something for your birthday. Unknowingly you told me what you wanted last night. I've never had such a lovely time as I had last week. If only I'd had a few more days maybe I could have helped you find your true feelings for me. You seem so very near to me now. Do you love your Don Juan just a teeny weeny bit?

Just as a flower seems to die, in reality the bulb is growing larger so that there will be a far more beautiful flower later on – so too my love for you seemed to die. But now it is far deeper and stronger than before. Somehow I can write no more. My heart is so full, the words which tumble from my mind would be just a jumbled mess. My dearest, I love you very, very much.

Goodbye for a short while,
Len

Joan and Len met several times after his return from Canada and before his next overseas posting. It is obvious from the letters that their relationship changed significantly. I wish I had talked to them about this while they were alive. Was Joan worn down by Len's persistence, or was there a specific time on leave together that clinched it?

*　*　*

A1 Flight, 2 Squadron
RAF Station
Heaton Park
Manchester
13th May 1942

My dearest Joan,

I wanted to see you again before I left but that was impossible. You know maybe you could overcome the feeling that we would not be happy together. I have your photo to look at, and there your eyes say "yes" but when I come home next time I wonder what they will say!

The food here is excellent and there's plenty of it. I'm stationed in a park. It's very beautiful – hills and valleys, lakes on which we can go boating and it's very fresh and clean. You'd love it here. Good night brown eyes. Write soon, dear, to your

　　Len

*　*　*

Manchester
18th May 1942

My Darling Joan,

It's now close upon midnight but before the train leaves London I must write down a few thoughts. How lovely it was to see you and speak to you. Somehow I seem to get strength from seeing you. I feel too that you are as happy as I am. Dearest, we have been so happy together haven't we. I'm frightened that this wonderful feeling might cease if we were married, but no it couldn't could it?

Joan dear, I love you so much. I will not post this letter till I get back to camp. So now I'll say goodnight. You'll be in your bed and I shall be in the corner seat of the train. Sleep tight sweetheart.

19th May 1942

Morning once more. We reached Manchester at 4.45. At the YMCA I met the rest of the boys except one who was caught by the police at Euston. I was also stopped at Euston, but it was just before midnight and as my pass was made out till midnight they couldn't do much about it though I was miles from my station. I arrived back at camp at 7.00 this morning, had breakfast and am now waiting to go on parade at 8.40am.

It has started to rain very hard so maybe the parade will be cancelled. At times the Air Force doesn't seem very keen to finish this war. We are free now from noon until 8.30 tomorrow morning. I feel we are still too free and easy.

Oh Joan my dear, what a wonderful letter you wrote me. We are just like a couple of kids. It's fun isn't it. We can always be like that can't we. Get away by ourselves now and then and leave the world to look after its own worries. I've just received a Christmas card which had been returned from America. I wonder if I'll ever get all of the letters back.

    Au revoir,

    Ever your Len

* * *

Manchester
22nd May 1942

My Very Dear Joan,
Today I have been reflighted and am now with the rest of my boys in A1 Flight 2 Squadron. I don't know what it is about them – they're a terrible crowd of fellows, always scrounging off something, but they're the grandest set of boys one could ever wish to be with. Also today I have been kitted out with khaki shorts, trousers, shirts and socks, and various other tropical kit. Everything of course is very hush hush but we're certainly not going to Iceland.

I borrowed Omar Khayyam from one of the boys and read it once again. He's a wise old bird, but I prefer Marcus Aurelius. I'm now going to read for an hour ("Black Narcissus") then go to supper.

Goodnight wishes from your
Len

* * *

Margate
1st June 1942

Joan Darling,
Did you manage to get any sleep last night? Dad came in to wake me up to go down to the dugout. I guess I must have been in a stupor. I just dozed off again. Somehow I thought it was our boys paying Jerry a visit!

Yes Joan, I feel you must be right in your ideal of love and marriage. Anything which falls short of that cannot be a real, deep and lasting love. Let's live and work for that ideal and realise it together. I feel that our friendship is almost as complete as it could be. Marriage which is to last for thirty or forty years must have its foundation in comradeship. Friendships last for years and years, but marriages are so often ruined after only a short time – why? Because the husband and wife are lovers rather that comrades. Yet as you say it is possible to be happily married and very much in love with each other after many, many years.

I am very much in love with a young girl, and I think she is with me, though she doesn't like to admit it. We are the greatest of friends. We both feel it wiser to wait till the end of the war before getting married. We have many things in common and many in which our opinions are opposed (at least we wouldn't be dull or lost for argument). Do you think, as I do, that we could be happy for ever if we were married? I know we would be always happy as friends. When the war is over we will both be older and wiser then we can make up our minds. Of course really there is only one mind to make up – even now.

Write to me soon Joan and tell me your thoughts and dreams. Remember I'm a dreamer too. God bless you, dearest, and keep you safe and well for
Your loving Len

* * *

Margate
4th June 1942

My Own Darling,
Looking back it seems as though I'd been with you for ages, but when I was with you, oh how quickly the precious hours flew by. And dearest, they were precious wonderful hours weren't they? There are just two things to do – to look back and remember the grand times

we've had together and to look forward, oh so eagerly to those happy days ahead. They <u>are</u> waiting for us – waiting till we're ready for them.

Here's that little verse:

> *Till we come to that day when our partings are over*
> *Till our hopes and our wishes come true,*
> *I shall carry the thrill of these days spent together*
> *And a future – all centred in you.*
> *Till the things that divide us for ever are ended*
> *And the troublesome days all depart*
> *In my thoughts, your dear face will be always beside me,*
> *Your love ever locked in my heart.*

Goodnight my dear. I feel somehow empty, but I know when I have your letter that all will be well again.

Len

Two other items were enclosed with this letter. This poem seems to have been written by Len, as he placed his initials after it:

> *I loved a maid with dark brown hair*
> *And hazel eyes had she.*
> *For love of her to far-off Eire*
> *I sadly went away.*
> *I toiled, I hoped, yet still I loved.*
> *My lonely years passed by.*

I toiled, I hoped, I prayed and then –
And then so rich was I.

One day I journeyed home again.
Saw Joan: came home to stay.
I found my love quite old and plain,
Old, yet the same sweet maid.

"Goodbye" she sighed, "forget me now.
No longer am I young."
"I loved your heart of gold you see
And not your youth" said I.

The following quote (attributed to Stephen Grellet) was made into a framed picture by Lovely and Son of Margate. It hung in the kitchen throughout my childhood and I still have it:

I shall pass through
this world but once.
Any good therefore
that I can do or any
kindness that I can
show to any human
being, let me
do it now.
Let me not defer
or neglect it, for

I shall not pass
this way again.

* * *

>Hut 3B, 3 Squadron
>2 Wing
>RAF Station
>West Kirby
>Cheshire
>10th June 1942

My Very Dear Joan,
In your last letters you said you had been day dreaming about me. These last few days I've been dreaming too, and planning. I've been to many places which you would love to see. I've been to Wales and Scotland, Canada, France and America, not to mention many places in England. I want you to come with me and see them all. Wouldn't it be grand, we'd have such fun. You would love these beautiful scenes and views even more than I do.

I never imagined I'd be like this, but I'm told love does strange things. I'm always thinking of what I can do for you, how I can make you happy. Joan, why did this have to happen to us now, when things around us are so uncertain. I don't think it is the war that has made this difference because I have met other girls and never felt like this about them – and you have met other boys and haven't felt with them the same as you do about me. My dear, don't be frightened of loving me. I know you have so much to give. The only way I can hurt you is by loving you too much and worrying about you. Joan, you do love me don't you – not in a wild passionate way, but with a deep feeling of comfort and security. That is how I love you. With you I feel I can face the world far better than before. So many of my hopes and ideals have come tumbling down.

> "But if the while I think on thee, dear friend,
> All ideals are restored and sorrows end."

Always I have wanted to just travel around and find a place by a stream and there to build a cabin. I could be far happier in a house I'd built myself than living in one for which I was just paying rent. I've dreamed too of having a boat and getting away from the bustle of life, of maybe finding an island. Always I seem to try to get away from crowds. I wonder if it is an unconscious fear that if I stayed in the town I'd lose my ideals. I told a girl my hopes and she said they were too high for this world. She said she had similar ones but they had just fallen to the ground through the wickedness of this world.

If you join the services, don't let them sit on you (they might squash you and that definitely would not be nice). When a crowd of girls or fellows get together it seems inevitable that their morals get disgustingly low and they forget themselves. Don't let them change you. Be good, sweet maid.

    Yours with love,
    Len x

Excerpt from his journal

We were posted to West Kirby on 10th June. We weren't here very long, just a week during which time Met and I went to Liverpool and W K to cinemas. Food was not so good and there was no possible chance of leave. On Thursday 18th June we boarded the *Stirling Castle*.

Len in RAF uniform

Len in his flying suit

Len in RAF uniform

Len wearing US flying gear in South Carolina, USA

Len in the cockpit, Oxford

Len and Harvard aircraft

Chapter Three

South Africa

"An animal called a camel-lion changes its colour..."
June 1942 – September 1943

A T this point, Len was in South Africa for pilot training. Joan was called up, and became a WAAF in Gloucestershire.

MF MF
HQ RAF
c/o APO 1945
16th June 1942

Joan,
Please tell me if you're lonely – let me know your troubles for it will help. Nobody can hope to be happy all the time. Yes dear – It would make a big difference if we

were engaged, it would seem to bind us to each other but surely our love is strong enough without that outward sign of a ring on your finger. It is the inward spiritual feeling that means so much. What do you feel?

We are going to South Africa and the voyage will probably take six weeks. We have an EFTS course which lasts 12 weeks and we do about 70 hours flying including instrument and night flying. Then there is an SFTS course lasting 24 weeks with 150 hours flying. Then we may remain out there or go to the Middle East. There's just a chance we may do Operational Training in England but that will probably be for married men. (I'm not dropping any hints dear.) Then we will get on to the real thing. I do miss you so much. We've just had a short glimpse of each other but I still believe in Destiny. I can't believe we just wander aimlessly through life.

You mention your vices but not by name. Of course you smoke now and again but I forgive you if you promise to eat a little more. Then you will put that horrible red ink on your finger nails. I much prefer the colourless varnish. However as you have already told me it isn't my business.

I'm glad my bed was comfortable, you have my full permission to use it whenever you like. Joking apart, Joan – it is very good of you to sleep there when Dad is fire-watching. I shall not forget that.

My Darling – do you really want us to be engaged? You have my ring and I have your photograph which means so much to me. I've just discovered that "reveille" is at 5.15 tomorrow – what an unearthly hour. Goodnight Sweetheart. Be brave – our love will help us both.

Len x

PS I enclose three soap coupons which I haven't used.

The ring Len mentioned is a small wooden ring which he made, together with a hinged wooden presentation box. Joan kept it and I still have it. Len was very good at woodwork and made many household items.

* * *

MFMF
4th July 1942

Joan my dearest,
I am writing this while still on the voyage but I don't think I will be able to send it until I disembark. I shall be glad when this voyage is over for the food is really poor and insufficient. The potatoes are all bad and quite a lot of other food has maggots in it which is not very appetising. If this is what we get, how do the poor devils in Libya exist.

On the first night out almost everyone was on deck in the moonlight singing songs of home – "Keep Right on to the End of the Road", "Bluebells of Scotland", traditional songs of the British Isles and then some hymns which were sung softly and with meaning. Then some [African-American] songs and hillbilly songs. It was wonderful – the moon shining on the water, voices echoing down and the ship steaming silently onwards. The night we arrived at the first port of call the songs were of a different nature. Rather happier and brighter than the first. These included "Holy City" and "Jerusalem" seeming to suggest one was glad and thankful for the safe voyage. Psychology at work, eh!

I've seen some flying fish – not at all like I expected. Quite small in fact and resembling sparrows rather than fish. The colour of the sea changes from green to bluish green and finally to a very deep royal blue. It's impossible to compare this last colour. One has to see it to believe it. When the sun shines on the spray made by the ship, miniature and momentary rainbows are formed. At night the stars are reflected in the dark water. It's fine Joan, but I think I preferred the North Atlantic trip. Maybe because then I wasn't quite so far away from home. This time I've really felt this parting. Before it was a new experience and I went off without a care. I now know how much it must have hurt Mum. I don't mean that I'm unhappy about it. No – it's just that now I do realise that I'm thousands of miles away. And yet Joan do you know I often feel you very close. Are you watching me perhaps.

I miss you oh so much. Almost every day my last thoughts are with you and on waking my thoughts are with you again. I think of the very happy times we've had and laugh at one or two misunderstandings. I thought a lot on your remark about our love (I dare to repeat <u>our</u> love) being born because of the war. I honestly don't think that is true of us. Rather should I hope and suggest that it happened in spite of the war. But as you also say "Time will tell". Well I don't mind waiting, for I know what the answer will be – don't you?

These are few words indeed aren't they, but one of these days I'll sit down and write a book for you. For a little while it's goodbye my dear from
    Your
    Len

* * *

                              MF MF
                              HQ RAF

My Own Darling,
Once again I have time to write a few lines to you. I heard the news last night and it wasn't very promising – the loss of Tobruk, a setback in Russia and serious losses in the Mediterranean. All very disappointing and there doesn't seem anyone to blame except the enemy.

Now I'll make your mouth water. I have been able to buy some jam – 9d a pound, condensed milk, salmon, tinned fruit etc. all without coupons. We weren't fortunate enough to have cabins or bunks so we have to put up with the usual hammocks though I've been lucky enough to get a mattress which I put on the bench where the hammocks are kept. Here I am very comfortable and I do have a hammock in case the ship starts rolling. Up till now it has been very steady compared to my return trip from Canada. I think when we go on our world trip in 1945 we'll go in June for it's not rough then.

This afternoon we commence lectures so the time should just fly along. I only hope the next twelve months will pass quickly – then maybe "I'll be with you in apple blossom time". I feel I must wait for a letter from you before I rewrite those letters of two years ago. You know my feelings, but I can only guess yours and now I'm not with you I'll have to rely on your letters. I think it rather wonderful that we both have the same conception of love. I read this a few weeks ago "Love is the forgetting of oneself in the interests of another".

Goodbye my dearest. God Bless you and keep you well and happy.

>Your ever loving
>Len

* * *

Airgraph
23rd July 1942

My Very Dear Joan,

What a long journey we've had and I'm sure we are very glad to be on terra firma once more. I have sent both you and Mum cables and I also wrote to you once a week while on the voyage. I learn that it will be a few months before your letters are sent on to me, but I must be patient. I will write a proper letter tomorrow – you'll probably get it about October.

Yesterday we were allowed out of camp for the first time and we thoroughly enjoyed ourselves. We had a really good meal. The town is very clean and modern but I think it has been spoilt by men in the services. There are plenty of silk stockings, shoes and other things difficult to obtain at home, but I expect I will be able to send you some.

I find it difficult to write what I'd like to. Our love seems to belong so very much to us that I don't like the thought of a third party knowing about it. So darling, don't worry. I love you and think of you always. Please remember me to your Mother, Gladys and Jack.

Au revoir my love,
Your Len

Airgraphs were about four inches wide and five inches long. A single page was reduced photographically to one quarter of the original size, making it quite hard to read. But transport by air rather than sea saved many weeks.

* * *

My Dear Joan,

You'll be envious when I tell you what I've been doing since I arrived in this country. I'll have to be careful just what I tell you for censorship is strict. As soon as we disembarked, we boarded a train and went out to a camp in the country. Here there is nothing but sand and we're sleeping in tents. This I find quite enjoyable and it reminds me of my scouting days. But unfortunately the food is exceptionally bad – and this in a country where it should be quite the opposite. So we usually go into town for a good meal as we are allowed out each day from 1 pm until midnight.

Durban I find is an extremely clean and modern city. Here I was able to send you a pair of stockings – unfortunately not pure silk, for there aren't any left. When you reply if you could send me measurements for your more flimsy garments I may be able to send you those too. There are many Indians here in Durban but of course a great number of natives still live in their villages and wear their native dress. This is a marvellous country and the climate the best I've experienced. It's winter now but it's lovely, warm and dry with a gentle breeze, but yesterday we had a mild sandstorm.

Met, Bob and I were in a cinema a few nights ago when a young married man invited us to his home for dinner. They have three small boys – I like the youngest best. They have a lovely home, Joan, with banana trees, orange and lemon trees and all sorts of things in the garden – doves, pigeons, guinea pigs, chickens, three dogs and a wonderful collection of small birds.

It's ages since I've had a letter from you so I have re-read those I have with me. One I have is the loveliest I've received in which you say how awful it seems that we should be parted so soon. You ask if being engaged would make a big difference. Yes sweetheart, I do think it would because we would belong to each other. You've given me something which I only dreamed existed. Love that I have for you can surely only come once. It's a beautiful happy feeling. To me all that is loving, honest, good, true and beautiful, all that is wonderful, kind and understanding is you, Joan. My one ambition is to finish my work here and come home to England and to you.

God Bless you and keep you safe and well for
    Your loving
    Len

* * *

MF MF
15th August 1942

Hello Darling,
I'm keeping very fit and strangely happy. It isn't wrong to be happy away from you is it? I think it is because of you that I feel this way.

ABSENCE, hear thou my protestation
Against thy strength,
Distance and length:
Do what thou canst for alteration,
For hearts of truest mettle
Absence doth join and Time doth settle.

Who loves a mistress of such quality,
His mind hath found
Affection's ground
Beyond time, place, and all mortality.
To hearts that cannot vary
Absence is present, Time doth tarry.

My senses want their outward motion
Which now within
Reason doth win,
Redoubled by her secret notion:
Like rich men that take pleasure
In hiding more than handling treasure.

By Absence this good means I gain,
That I can catch her
Where none can watch her,
In some close corner of my brain:
There I embrace and kiss her,
And so enjoy her and none miss her.

I still read our sonnets fairly often. As you wrote in one of your letters "they seem so essentially to belong to us."

We are still at the same camp somewhere in South Africa and it seems we will be here for a while as the flying schools are full. I feel sure I shall never do any flying much less fighting in this war. In which case, am I to be glad and thankful or sorry? I expect when the time comes I shall be just as eager as I was when I joined this outfit.

Life here is very pleasant – too easy I fear, so that we tend to forget the war which now more than ever must be won. We are allowed out nearly every day from 1 pm until midnight. And almost every day we go to dinner at Mr Ridsdale's house. It is almost as though I was in my own home. I have a bath any time I like, listen to the wireless or play the piano. (Hot water is unattainable in camp.) They have three small boys. The youngest is not quite able to feed himself. Can you imagine "Uncle Len" feeding him and playing with him? I can hardly believe it myself and I love doing it.

I usually wear shorts and am getting quite brown. It's lovely to be out in the air as we are and sleeping in tents. After the war I must find a job in the open air. I have been thinking about a chicken farm. In peace time it should be a paying concern and it doesn't seem to require very much knowledge to rear chickens.

Cheerio my darling. Write to me soon. In the press about a week ago, it stated that a mail ship had sunk. It seems that the mail from England was on board.

Au revoir

Yours with love

Len x

The poem in the letter is an ode by John Donne entitled *"That time and absence proves rather helps than hurt to loves."* I love the fact that my parents discussed poetry and books and music rather than focusing on the war.

* * *

In Transit
20th August 1942

My Darling Joan,

My first news is to tell you that in about 6 weeks' time you should receive 2 sets of lingerie or underclothes or whatever you call them. My one fear is that you will be offended. Please don't dear. My love comes with them to you for Christmas. Secondly I'm still happy and well. Have you joined up yet? Be always as you were when I left. I'll be thinking of you sweetheart and love you always. I've been out on one or two trips to the country. It's grand here, Joan. Hundreds of hills and valleys – beautifully green and rugged. There's something about hills that grips, isn't there. Unfortunately I'm not allowed to tell you about this country in detail, but later on I hope to do so.

    Au revoir dear,
    Your Len

* * *

MFMF
3rd September 1942

Joan Dear,

In this letter I'll just run over a few points about the country. I think it's the climate which I like, especially in the evening. After a good downpour of rain it's lovely to see everything looking fresh and green. It certainly rains here. Our tent was flooded the other night and we all felt very miserable when we had to dress at 4.30am.

    Everywhere you look there are hills. Fold upon fold of hills – narrow, winding steep roads, picturesque valleys and pretty streams and rivers. On Sunday Met and I were taken to the Native Reserve. The natives don't seem to be treated very well. Some of them are definitely no good at all (just as there are some white men like that), but the majority of the natives seem to be friendly decent human beings.

    We have got quite used to sleeping on sand. It gets everywhere – in kit, blankets, hair. But how ever bad conditions are it is always possible to think of some other poor fellows and have pity on them. Why should we grumble.

Roll on the time when I can see you again, to see that face, those hands and to hear that voice I love so much.

Au revoir my dear
>   Yours as ever,
>   Len

* * *

> RAF Wing
> 75 Air School
> Lyttleton
> Pretoria
> Transvaal
> South Africa
> 21st September 1942

Darling,

I'm happy once again. I've had another letter from you posted on 16th July. The latest I've had from Dad was posted on August 6th. He said you had received my cable telling you of my safe arrival in South Africa. So you've been down to Hastings and I'm glad you had a good time. Yes I have seen the "little church in the wood". Maybe you saw my name in the visitors book. I do hope you went to Fairlight Glen. It would be lovely in July.

We arrived here yesterday after a very comfortable journey. We passed through marvellous country and my camera was doing overtime. Photography is rather an expensive hobby but it's the only one I indulge in here. The meals on the train were quite good and the beds excellent. Imagine sleeping between sheets for the first time since June 9th when I was at Heaton Park.

Au revoir my dear,
Len

Joan and Len eventually retired to Fairlight near Hastings in East Sussex in 1983 and often enjoyed walking in Fairlight Glen.

* * *

Pretoria
28th September 1942

Joan Dearest,
We have been here a week now and are getting used to the routine and are now training under the South African Air Force. This of course entails the learning of their drill and various or perhaps I should say numerous rules. This is my fourth Air Force. I'm becoming quite an international airman.

We came here full of hopes to get cracking on a course. We might have known that a disappointment awaited us. It looks as though I shall be here six weeks before I do anything. Oh and something else – Met and I are not in the same flight now. Do you think I'm grumbling Joan? Well maybe I am, but I think I have cause to do so – just waiting around and doing nothing. I'm fed up with it. But don't tell Mum, will you. I know this mood will pass. I can usually accept the inevitable so things like this pass over my head. The trouble is the same thing happens time and time again.

On Saturday I went to Johannesburg and had a very enjoyable time. It's a grand city full of life, especially at night with all the bright lights. I bought Mum some stockings for Christmas. I should like to send cigarettes for Dad but the duty is far too much.

The country here is very different from Natal. Here it's one high plateau about five or six thousand feet above sea level. The people too are different. In Natal they were either of British descent or pro-British. Here there are numerous people of German and Dutch descent. There are many who do not want this war and many more who are definitely opposed to it. Moreover they resent the presence of British troops. But the majority are kind hospitable people. There are big political problems to be solved here. We have been told it is nothing to do with us and not to talk politics.

Au revoir, my love. I'm thinking of you and wishing I was with you.

    Always yours,
    Len

***

Pretoria

Dear Joan,

Here at Lyttleton we commence work in earnest once more. Reveille is at 05.45 hrs and lights out is at 22.15 hrs. Lectures, P.T. and Drill occupy the hours in between. The meals here are good, which is a blessing. After this course we hope to have three weeks leave and this I will probably spend at Klorf in Natal with Mr & Mrs Hopewell. They have been very kind to Met and myself.

The last day out at our last station Met and I went to lunch in town at a services club. This was a delightful cold meat and salad followed by fruit and ice cream. This cost the great sum of 1/-. I hope I'm making you envious. Then we went to the cinema – called "Ye Olde Playhouse" which is built in Tudor style. If you look up to the ceiling you see stars and clouds passing overhead which is a wonderful effect. There was a special concession to the military (that's us) and we got in for 1/3. After the cinema we had a mixed grill of sausages, kidney, a chop, piece of steak, chips and tomatoes for 3/6. Met had beer and yours truly had his usual cider. I must admit I was extravagant that day but I thoroughly enjoyed myself. You don't blame me do you?

I'm getting used to being abroad now. It's wonderful to be able to travel and I know I'm very lucky but there's no place like home – to be with friends and those one loves.

Goodbye my love until next week.
 Your
 Len

* * *

Pretoria
6th October 1942

Hullo Joan,
We have now been here for two weeks and have done nothing in connection with flying training. True we've done plenty of drill, PT and rifle drill. Also we've had some topical and history lectures about South Africa. These I found most interesting and should prove helpful in the future in understanding the people here. South Africa has two peoples – the British and Afrikaners; two languages – English and Afrikaans (there are also many native languages); two capitals – Pretoria the administrative capital, and Cape Town the legislative capital where parliament sits. There are two groups of people – the pro-British and the anti-British. So you can see how difficult it is to govern out here. It appears that there are three big parties opposed to the Government. They are also opposed to each other, which is a good thing as they are not strong enough for a rebellion.

I haven't had any letters from you since 16th July. But I received a Christmas card from Gladys which had been sent to Canada. Don't send any letters by air mail out here, for it takes as long as ordinary mail. But airgraphs are faster.

Tomorrow I do an Aptitude Test. They make use of the information like a kind of psycho-analysis and are able to say if a candidate will be able to fly bombers or fighters.

I wish you could be out here to enjoy all the things I'm seeing.

Au revoir, my love.

Yours, Len

Len was always interested in languages. At the back of his journal he compiled a dictionary of Afrikaans words with their English meanings.

* * *

Pretoria
15 October 1942

Joan dear,
It's now time to write to you once more so I'm feeling very bright and cheerful. I often think when I'm writing that you are here and then when I've finished you say au revoir. It's then that I miss you so much.

I'll tell you something about the natives. They are definitely the underdog here though I'm happy to note that the Britishers usually treat them well, and as servants not as slaves. There are strong bodies working for the natives trying to get them a better deal. Unfortunately the Afrikaner remembers that the natives not so many years ago used to steal his cattle and kill his women and children. Also they have to be suppressed a little for there are a lot of poor white people who are little better than natives. It must never do for the natives to be above the whites. This of course is the view out here (not mine). I've found a great number of natives very well educated and living up to the Western standard of civilisation. They of course speak English as well as their own language. But of course there's the unpleasant side to it. In the native kraals especially disease is rampant and their morals are disgusting low (once more compared with civilized Europe). There is a tremendous colour bar. To be seen talking with natives is to be considered not quite right in the head, and sexual intercourse between white and coloured people is a civil and military offence with very heavy punishment. I saw the film "Rhodes of Africa". He spoke of the natives as children. That's just what they are Joan – children to be loved and taught the better ways of life. This colour bar is the worst thing about Africa and it will take a long to time stamp it out.

I enclose a cutting from the "Outspan", a weekly magazine about the elections here. Do you realise that if the opposition or Nationalists become the governing body – as they may well do – this country will declare peace with Germany, become a neutral and we shall probably be interned. Sounds bad. It is for that very reason that I think we are having rifle training. So though I don't see any fun in the air, I may on the ground.

I'll write again next week. I am still on guard duty. Had hoped to have Saturday and Sunday off but that's been cancelled now. Goodbye for a little while.

Always yours with love,
Len x

Excerpt from his journal
<u>Lyttleton 75 Air School</u>
Arrived here about 9.30 on 21st Sept 42 (Monday). Camp very well laid out. Food a lot better than Clairwood. Allowed out one evening per week. Johannesburg about 40 miles away. Pretoria about 7 miles away. Anti RAF feeling in camp as far as some officers are concerned. Plenty of "Bull–t". Tried to shake us but failed (as usual). Waited for 1 month at I.T.W. during which time I did 1 weeks duty of guard. Then posted to A.T.W. on 17th October 1942.

* * *

Airgraph from Joan

70C219
TO: 1334965 LA/C MANWARING L.C.G.
PUPIL PILOTS MESS
3 AIRSCHOOL, WONDERBOOM
P.O. BOX 919. PRETORIA
TRANSVAAL
SOUTH AFRICA

7 Kent Road
Margate
18th October 1942

My dear Len,
I had three lovely letters from you today – it made you seem very close to me. I do write to you every week Len, even if you don't always get them, remember that I do write.

We are all keeping well. Your mother had two letters from you so she is on top of the world. Mrs Mack is a bit annoyed because your mother lent her "Brave New World" by Huxley. Remember it? It made me laugh when she told me. I've just been trying to explain that it isn't as bad as they think and it will probably do them good to read it. Don't you think so.

I'll write a long letter in answer to yours tomorrow. I hope this will reach you quickly to let you know we miss you so much and think of you very often.

Au revoir. My love, Joan

* * *

Pretoria
8th November 1942

Joan dear,

It is Sunday once more. In the truest sense of the words it is a day of rest here. I usually get up at 8 o'clock on Sundays have breakfast then write a letter, maybe read a book and do some washing. This morning I had to go to church parade.

A few days ago we were on the veldt just outside the camp doing signals with the Aldis lamps. All went well till someone disturbed a snake among the rocks. The signals were forgotten though the instructor three hundred yards away was still sending out signals. The snake went back into the rocks and the cruel boys lit a fire in the hope of smoking it out, by which time the snake was probably a long way away for we never saw it again.

I now have 100 photographs taken in South Africa. They will make an impressive reminder of my stay out here. I must stop writing now to mend some socks and to do a little Theory of Flight and Armaments. Maybe after all Sunday isn't a complete day of rest.

Now it is time to say au revoir to my little girl. Is she still little or eating a bit more and putting on some weight?

    Cheerio my dear,
    Your loving Len.

Len collected commercial postcards of native tribes and wild animals as well as taking photographs.

***

**Christmas and New Year
Greetings**

Pretoria
16th November 1942

From Somewhere in Africa
This Christmas and New Year
To all at home I'm wishing
Victory, Peace and Good Cheer!

My Own Darling,
Here's wishing you all the best for Christmas and the New Year. Please remember me to your Mother, Gladys and Jack. War news seems better for us. Let's hope it will soon be over.

Wings across the ocean bringing
Let us hope we'll be together
Greetings kind and true.
In a not far distant day.

Breezes in the trees are whispering
Together – and for ever!
My loving thoughts of you.
Oh hasten, Lord, that day.

Goodbye for a little while dear. Have a good time.

Keep your chins up – friends in Blighty!
Keep your thumbs up – hold them tightly,
But chiefly keep those home fires burning
For pretty soon I'll be returning!

All my love,
Len

* * *

Pretoria
18th November 1942

Hullo dear,
I received my first airgraph last week so now I'm hoping for more. I have now started my course and Met and I are once more in the same flight. I had a good weekend in Jo'burg with the boys. I wonder if there was anything you particularly wanted for your 21st birthday? I already had something in mind and on Saturday I saw it and got it while the opportunity was there. I will send it at the end of the month.

We are beginning to have really hot weather. I dread to think what it's like down in Durban. If I have leave for Christmas I expect I shall go down that way. And now how are you? And have you yet joined the services or the factory?

One night last week I read all your letters that I have with me. I took over an hour. I found something new in most of them which I had not noticed before. Au revoir for now dear. Write soon to

>Your loving
>Len

* * *

>Pretoria
>24th November 1942

Joan dear,

Mum has received her first parcel. Have you received stockings and underclothes yet? Let me know if there was any duty to pay. I think it would be better for Ron if you told him it was all over. Seems pointless continuing a friendship that will hurt you both. When you leave Margate don't give him your address. Drastic but I imagine effective. Have just heard that I have passed all my exams. Thank goodness I'll be leaving this place soon. The fed up feeling has reached me at last.

Au revoir my love.
>Love from Len

* * *

Pupil Pilots Mess
PO Box 919
Pretoria
Transvaal
South Africa
30th November 1942

Hullo Dear,

Here is my promised letter telling you about the native dancing. Mr Roberts took us in his car to the gold mine. The natives from the compound have dances from time to time. Their energy is boundless. All sorts of tribes – Bantus, Swazis, Zulus, Basutus – many more I can't remember from West Africa, some from East Africa, more from Belgian Congo. Unfortunately they aren't allowed to wear native dress or carry arms, but they make a very good show out of odd bits of material. They don't wear shoes or boots so maybe you can imagine what a pitch of frenzy they arouse in themselves when I tell you that with their bare feet they dig holes in the ground which I couldn't do with boots. It's amazing. All their dances portray something in their life and are very deep in meaning and full of ceremony. There was a native fellow acting as commentator. He was extremely witty and seems to have the average Englishman very well taped up. He said there were three times: GMT, South Africa time and Native time, which was anything from two to three hours behind the other two.

We started flying again yesterday. There are just minor differences here, such as a landing speed which is 5 mph faster than it was in England. It takes longer to climb owing to the slightly rarefied atmosphere. This morning we were doing spins and lost height very quickly. I did six spins and those were on an empty stomach. I had a very hearty breakfast at 9 o'clock.

Now I will say au revoir.

Yours with love,

Len x

* * *

Margate
9 November 1942

Len dear,

I'm punctual for our date today. I'm on holiday this week and I'm having such a lazy time. I've just been for a piano lesson. I'm working on a simplified version of Handel's *Largo* and the *Blue Danube*, though I doubt if you'd recognise them as yet.

I went to a dance with Ernie on Saturday at Dreamland. He dances well and we had a good time. And as an example of what love does to you, Gladys is learning to dance. Jack came down for 48 hrs this weekend. He's getting terribly thin, he's all bone. I think he'll be better when he gets over his vaccinations and inoculations.

This airgraph is all about us. How are you? Your letters have stopped again so I'm hoping to get several next week. I hope work is going alright and I'll understand if you don't have time to write as often.

Au revoir, dear Len.
Your Joan

*　*　*

Pretoria
26th December 1942

My Dear Joan,

On Boxing Day twelve months ago I landed in England, so I thought I would write to you on that happy anniversary. In one of your letters you want me to be happy. Well I am almost as happy as I was this time last year. I've had such a lovely Christmas, but it is so hot I think I'd prefer the snow and to huddle round a large fire.

On Christmas Eve Met and I went to a dance in the WAAF camp. The girls were allowed to wear evening dresses and most of them were lovely. We had all the usual dances and one or two extra ones (Afrikanese). Ices and light refreshments were served and I was really sorry when midnight ended the dance.

For Christmas Day we had all the good things imaginable. Breakfast was the same – porridge, eggs and bacon, but the dinner was really the "tops". Soup, fish, beef, pork and turkey, vegetables, fruit salad, ice cream, fresh fruit including oranges, bananas, peaches and plums, then cheese, nuts and sweets, tea or coffee, and beer and mineral water. About 9 or 10 courses I think.

Sorry I forgot of course we also had Christmas pudding. In the afternoon a crowd of us went for a walk down to the river. It was very pleasant beneath the trees.

I promised to tell you about the pests of this place. There are the usual flies and some very large beetles, about four times the size of the largest in England. There are grass hoppers – very pretty colours they are too – and locusts. The real terror of the insect world seems to be the scorpion, and thank goodness I haven't seen many of those. There are plenty of snakes, though only small ones, also lizards by the hundreds and an animal called a camel-lion. It is very much like a lizard. It lives on flies which it catches with its tongue which are almost as long as the animal itself. The camel-lion though usually green changes its colour to the same as its surroundings. Put it on something brown, the camel-lion changes to brown, put it on something white and it changes to that colour.

I will say au revoir now darling and write to you again soon.

>All my love,
>Len
>x (because of the Christmas spirit)

We are now all so familiar with exotic animals due to the marvellous wildlife programmes on television. But seventy years ago, most people had no idea about such creatures. Len was obviously fascinated by the chameleon.

* * *

Margate
7 January 1943

My Dear Len,

I had two airgraphs from you yesterday, also your Mum and Dad had one each. In mine you said you had not as yet heard from me that I had received your parcels. I hope you'll have heard from me by now, for I've thanked you in several letters. In case you haven't, may I thank you again? I received both the undies and the stockings within a few days of each other. I love them. I tried them all on the night I got them in front of an admiring audience consisting of Mum and Gladys. I showed them to your mother, and let your father just have a peep at the colours. Then I packed them away till Christmas, though I did take a peep now and then. They fit beautifully except that they were a wee bit on the large size. I soon remedied that. I wore them Christmas day – or some of them – for the first time. I always knew you had good taste, though I didn't think it went as far as undies. I tried to be annoyed at you for sending them, but I couldn't be. No more news.

Au revoir.
My love,
Joan

* * *

Pretoria
9th January 1943

My Dear Joan,

First of all I must tell you what a wonderful time Met and I had on our leave in Jo'burg. We stayed with Mrs Healey who said she was pleased to have us as her son is a prisoner of war in Italy. We went to a show, had a dance, played table tennis and cards and went for a drive round the city. It really is beautiful. All the houses are detached and the gardens too are very beautiful. We were very lazy on New Year's Day. I was sorry when we had to come back to Wonderboom, especially as we had two exams on the Monday.

During the past two weeks we have had six exams, two of which were real blighters. I got 46% for one exam and I was fairly near the top of the class. Some fellows got 12% and one only managed 5%. How terrible is that. On Monday we start night flying and also have to practise three times next week on the Link Trainer – the aeroplane that doesn't fly. On Friday I was able to get up to 4000ft and do loops, spins etc. So far I've done twenty eight spins and nine loops, a third of which have been done while flying solo.

I had an airgraph from your Mother. I have written to her and she should have received a food parcel I sent in November. No doubt <u>you</u> will gobble up most of the chocolate in it. I like this country more and more. I'm getting used to the heat now, but at the moment I am itching from mosquito bites. Last night I saw "Safari" in the camp cinema. Every time we see England in the cinema, the boys go almost mad with cheering. Which seems to point to the fact that there is only <u>one</u> country in this world.

So now dear Joan it is time to say au revoir again. Good luck and keep smiling.

.-/.-../.-..//--/-.--//.-../---/...-/.//

Len x

The Morse Code message reads "All my love". I do not know Morse Code but nowadays you can get an instant translation on the internet.

* * *

Pretoria
17th January 1943

My Dearest Joan,
How are you dear? I hope very well and happy as I am. Work is still going on nicely though it's rather heavy at the moment. Let's hope you will soon finish traveling around and work at Margate once more. I have some bad news but this I haven't told Mum. Six more of our boys, my pals from the old *Letitia* have been killed, and another badly injured in a crash. It seems tragic to think of all these boys have been through and now they are no longer here. As yet I haven't sent your cosmetics but they will come soon.

Au revoir, sweetheart.

Yours with love, Len x

* * *

Margate
21 January 1943

Len dear,
I had to write and thank you for the cable you sent for my birthday. It was the loveliest present I had. I had a lovely day, though we are having my "birthday tea" today. We've actually got a jelly. Your Mother and Father gave me a lovely present (protest was useless) – a collection of Mansfield's poems and a novel of Conrad, both bound in fawn leather. Mum gave me a wristwatch band. Gladys some ear-rings – you've never seen me in ear-rings have you – Henry a dress ring.
    Thank you again for your lovely thought.
    Au revoir. My love, Joan

It is amazing to think that something as humble as a jelly, normally associated with children's parties, should be such a cause for celebration and excitement.

* * *

Pretoria
31st January 1943

My Dear Joan,
Glad you received and liked the undies. Hope by now you have also had your 21st birthday gift. During the past 2 weeks we have been busy, but now I only have 3 more night flights left. Gee will I be glad when they're over.

My pals from another station flew over here yesterday but unfortunately I was up flying on a cross country trip. Hope to see them next week when I go to their station. My native boy would like to write to Mum. Would you also like to have a letter from him? He's a scrounging little devil but very likeable. At the moment he's saving his money to send his young brother to school in Rhodesia. Some evenings he's very talkative and I thoroughly enjoy listening to his adventures. He wants a photograph of Mr Churchill.

"Fare thee well for I must needs be gone." (Shakespeare!) Goodnight my love.

Len x

* * *

Margate
21 February 1943

My Dear Len,
I had an airgraph from you last week. You sounded so happy in it as though you were bubbling over, it cheered me up just reading it. I was feeling a little depressed at the time. I still don't know whether I've been accepted into the Forces or not. I had to see another doctor and yesterday my left shoulder was X-rayed – just to see if it's OK. It seems ridiculous because I've never had any trouble or pain in my shoulder. Still, I shall know definitely on Friday.

Goodnight dear. Please take care of yourself.

My love, Joan

*   *   *

Pretoria
1st February 1943

Hello Darling,

Thank you once again for the airgraph and also for your Christmas cable. Today I heard that I have passed one final exam, but I expected to pass that. It's Navigation we are all worried about. The paper was a proper devil. Also I have passed my final flying test at this station and today I did quite well on the Link. What a long time this course is taking. "Slow but sure" is the watchword – or perhaps as Met says "Very slow and not so sure." Today I completed my sixth and final Cross Country flight. I really enjoy them, we fly at about 2000ft and map read the whole time. The only snag is when an entry has to be made in the log the jolly old kite will not keep steady. On these trips we pay social calls to our pals at other stations. I have one more night flight left, about 3 hours formation flying, a spot of low flying and instrument flying and then I've finished this course.

Au revoir, dear. Please remember me to your Mother, Gladys and Jack.

Yours as ever,
Len

*   *   *

Margate
4 March 1943

My dear Len,
Received an airgraph from you yesterday dated 10/2/43. It's a good idea to number them. I've had them all except numbers 3 and 6, the last was number 7. I'd love to have a letter from your native boy – does he write English? What's his name? He sounds a likeable boy, there aren't many who bother about a younger brother's schooling. Do try and take a snap of him and send it to me. We've got one of George's native servant when he was out there but he was quite an old man, very upright and dignified looking. We're having glorious weather here. I hope it lasts.
   Write soon.
      Yours ever, Joan

* * *

Pupil Pilots Mess
21 Air School
Kimberley
Cape Province
South Africa
3rd March 1943

Hello Joan,
I have written thanking you for your letters but I'm afraid most of yours have been lost or delayed. Dad said

that you had passed your medical exam. What was all the trouble about anyway?

I can tell you a few things about these aeroplanes. Instead of a stick these kites have a wheel to control them. After a while on the ground I imagine myself driving a car. There are two throttles. To turn the right open the left-hand throttle and vice versa. A few days ago I was blind flying – that is flying by instruments only. And then the rain came and my instructor told me to take the shield away from my face and fly normally. It was raining so hard I literally could not see a thing, and as I had been flying on instruments for the previous half-hour I had no idea where I was. Luckily the shower soon passed and the instruments took over and landed. Two days ago while by myself I attempted to make a forced landing and found the retractable undercarriage wouldn't come down. So back to base I came and this time it was OK when I landed.

A couple of evenings ago I read a light novel about a young couple who decide to get away from city life. This takes place in the Scottish Highlands and gives a very good description of the beauty of the countryside. Now that's just what I want to do. Could I ask you to come with me? Would you come with me? I always feel the civilisation causes so much unhappiness. We should have lived one or two centuries ago with the pioneers. The book is "David and Joanna" by George Blake.

I've been down to Kimberley this afternoon and got the book you told me about. Of course I haven't read it yet, but as no-one yet has come back from the dead how can we know what happens when we leave this present life. However I'll read the book with an unbiased mind as I too am striving after Truth. Darling, just listen a minute. As long as we are happy in this life and make other people happy, what does it matter what form of life there is beyond. Don't let us try to find out what it is. Let us be happy and true and good while we can. I feel there must be some life after this, for otherwise there is no sense in us being here at all. But oh! how wonderful it would be to go on forever as you say completing each other and becoming greater in knowledge of truth.

My dear Joan, do you really weigh only 7st 9lbs. Do take care of yourself. You should weigh at least 9st. Why not try eating <u>two</u> pieces of bread and butter.

Goodnight my dear,
    Love from
    Len

* * *

Margate
22 March 1943

My dear Len,
I'm writing this in the twilight – the last few minutes before we put up the blackout and shut away the day. I've had my final

interview and I'm to be called up within 6 weeks. I'm going to be a "wireless transmitter". I've bought a book on Morse and I mean to try a little tapping out on the piano before I go. Jack has passed his driving test. I'm so pleased for him. We are hoping he will come home on leave next week. Henry is home this week. I'm glad I'll be seeing them both before I go.

Goodnight.

My love, Joan

* * *

Kimberley
15th April 1943

My Own Darling,

I call you that because I feel more fully than ever that we belong to each other. Maybe you can imagine how happy I am to have another letter from you. This one was posted on 24 November. It's such a lovely letter I don't mind if I don't have any for a long time now – oh yes I do – I want many more. You will know by now that all being well I shall be a Bomber pilot. At any rate I'm flying twin-engined planes now.

To answer another of your queries, an Afrikaner is one of the old foretrekkers or descendants of same – the Boers, though they mustn't be called Boers now. Actually they are a mixture of Dutch, German and some English. Throughout the generations they gradually built up their own language and customs and today form a large proportion of the South African nation. Unfortunately quite a number of Afrikaners still sing the hymn of hate against England. This of course has a lot to do with the anti-British feeling, especially in the Orange Free State and the Transvaal. I must point out that the Afrikaner is a fine fellow. If only the Boer War could be forgotten all would be well.

I've heard hundreds of love stories and they all seem so alike. Why is it that our story, our love is so different, more beautiful, deeper! Is it because we both know what we want and are both determined to reach that goal? Do you know Joan, whenever I see beauty or feel peaceful I always think of you and picture you sharing it with me. By the time I come home I expect you will be in the WAAFs. If you can give proof that your fiancé has returned from overseas you can have leave. Joking apart dear, could you be my fiancée (just) so that we could have leave together.

Now, returning to our earlier discussion about religion, I will give you my own conception of life and after. Our life begins on this earth and we reach a certain standard of knowledge and truth. God, the Creator and Father of everything, helps when we go astray, but so that we will not rely solely on Him, He has given us free will. Things were getting in a pretty mess so he sent Jesus Christ – his son – his prophet or what you will – to tell the people of the earth the truth of God. When we die our souls, spirits or mental beings pass to another place, there we are much nearer God and there we have infinitely more knowledge. There is no such place as Hell, but for those of us who have not been all that we could have been on this earth, we wait till we are mentally suited to go into the next world. From there as we progress we become more pure, more nearly like God so we progress from sphere to sphere. I have always said it doesn't matter in what manner one worships God on this earth so long as we do believe and have some ideal to attain. By this we are fitting ourselves for the next world.

I have something worrying me. I've spoken to Dad about it and he told me not to worry. It's what to do when the war is over. I know there is always the Library to go back to, but it seems overpowering now. There are many things I would like to do but they don't seem practicable. I don't put a great deal of value on wealth, but money is so necessary, isn't it? Woman is the power behind man, so woman give this man some power and some thought.

    Love from your
    Len

* * *

Margate
6 April 1943

My dear Len,

I'm sending an airgraph this week instead of a letter. I'm going to and fro to Hastings every day and I leave you to imagine how much time I have for writing letters, even to you.

I hope you're keeping well. We all are here, though your mother hasn't been too well. She had a nasty cold, and almost lost her voice. She is much better now. She has just finished making herself a dress and jacket, she's very proud of it. It's in a glamorous grassy green (alliteration intended) – you'd love it.

By the way, green is my favourite colour. Did "instinct" guide you to get my birthday present in green. I'm glad you did anyway. Your mother tells me green is your favourite colour too – I didn't know. Goodnight dear. I haven't time to write what is in my thoughts – perhaps in yours too.

Love,
Joan

* * *

Kimberley
23rd April 1943

My Dearest Joan,
Guess what I did last Sunday afternoon? I collected all my mail together and found that have 39 letters from you and 8 airgraphs. I read through all of them and felt so different afterwards, do you remember what you wrote I wonder. Sometimes you were very loving, and told me your deepest secrets, in others you were annoyed with me, but in all of them it was Joan behind those written words. I love you my darling.

I'd love to travel along anywhere, stopping in different places until I came to one that suited me. There I would settle down, build me a house and plant my own food. Ah well dreams, dreams my boy, come back to earth. How are all the folks at home – remember me to Henry and Jack and I do hope that you are or were able to see them before you are/were called up. Write soon.

Love,
Len

It must have been so hard to maintain a relationship under those circumstances. They were thousands of miles apart with no idea when or if they would meet again. Letters took much longer than airgraphs, so responses were often out of sync. Then there were the ongoing pressures and uncertainties of the war and the deprivations of daily life.

* * *

Kimberley
1st May 1943

My Dear Joan,
All this week we have been having exams and we are doing more night flying so we have been kept on our toes. I had another letter from you written on 25th January and an airgraph sent on 6th April. So you have also been very busy. I should hate travelling all that way every day.

Mum tells me you've had a mild winter so I imagine spring must be very beautiful in England now. Here we are just about having winter and the weather has been most severe. We've been grounded for two days, though usually we fly in all weathers. All seasons are nice in England. I imagine autumn will be very pleasant. It's so beautiful just when the leaves are changing colour.

Don't forget to send me a photograph of my Joan in uniform.

Au revoir, my dear.

Yours always,

Len x

* * *

Kimberley
8th May 1943

My Dear Joan,

This week I've had another letter from you containing the sample of material for your house coat. My dear young woman, when do you imagine you're going to wear it! You're in the WAAF, not the South African WAAF. I didn't think WAAFs had any leisure moments. In any case, in your spare time you'll be off down to town with the rest of the girls. I like the colour and imagine it will look very nice when made up. I'm so glad you were able to see Jack and Henry before you went. I expect you will be fairly busy for the first two months, so don't worry if you don't feel like writing any letters.

Did I tell you we've started night flying again? Believe me, it gets quite cold at night especially in the air so we make full use of the heaters in the aircraft. I have passed my formation flying test. The instructor who took the test was very pleased and said it was above average. I have also done an instrument flying cross country trip. In this, one flies entirely on instruments. A shield covers everything up except the instruments. So the ground cannot be seen. We then set off and fly on three different courses and noting the time and speed etc. we should arrive back over the base aerodrome. I was a little to the left and this was after flying for 1½ hours.

Love from
Len

* * *

Kimberley
29th May 1943

My Dear Joan,
This week we've been flying far more than we used to. On Tuesday I took up my first passenger. This was for a flight of 250 miles. It was in a mild sense a thrill and certainly a new sense of responsibility. Today I did another 250 mile trip, but my co-pilot was flying and I was navi-

gator. In order to take drifts one has to crawl down into the nose of the aircraft to use the instrument. It's easy for me to do it because I'm small, but some fellows have an awful job getting down and worse still getting back.

Today I had a letter from Met having an easy time in East London waiting for a course to commence. Says he hopes to have another 21 days leave. I received airgraphs from Mum saying you now have your uniform and expected to be moved again. Shall be very pleased to have a photograph. It's so long since I saw you, you might have changed. Maybe you're even more attractive and beautiful. Anyway dear it is a long time and I do miss you so much.

>Always your own
>Len

* * *

>Kimberley
>11 June 1943

My Dear Joan,
Your letter (15.3.43) made me so happy. I'm glad you're happy too, Joan. It doesn't do for us to be happy all the time for then life would be so monotonous and boring. It's the little "ups" and "downs" that make life worthwhile. But then you know that, so why am I philosophising about it.

You ask about the insects here. Yes there are spiders – quite big ones about as big as dogs. At night we hear lions roaring and the natives beating tom-toms and singing blood curdling songs of liberation. I enclose plans of four houses and rough sketch of two of them. I've got names for them too. Oh and children – yes I've names for children as well. If I had a boy I would call him Ian, Anthony, Michael or David – and if I had a girl I would call her Anne, Helen, Pauline or Jean.

Sorry to disappoint you Joan but I'm not very fond of liver so I probably wouldn't have enjoyed your effort. However it's a step in the right direction. I remember once you told me that your husband would have to live on tinned food for the first three months. Well at least there's some hope for the poor devil now. Just in passing, did you like the liver and bacon?

This afternoon I've been out on a reconnaissance and also taking aerial photographs. Now I have to write a report. Think I'll leave it till Sunday – I'm too lazy.

Au revoir dear, write again soon to your
    Loving
    Len

* * *

Kimberley
19th June 1943

My Dear Joan,

It's Saturday once more and time to write to you again. I've just woken up from an afternoon nap. I was flying last night so feel a little tired. This past week I have been flying more than ever. I have been on two more reconnaissance trips and my co-pilot and I have finished one section of our bombing programme. Last night I went on a cross country flight. A Captain came with me and he produced some sandwiches and remarked we might just as well make ourselves comfortable. So there we sat eating sandwiches. He fell asleep just before we reached our objective. We returned and asked for permission to land. Bags of panic! The Aerodrome Control Officer wouldn't let us, though I couldn't see why not. There were no other planes around. However I went round again and this time it was OK.

The Wings Exam results are out and I passed all of them. What happens next is in the laps of the Gods. I don't really mind as long as I see you soon. It's such a long time now. Next week I hope to go to the big city and do some more shopping – this time to get something for my Mother and a WAAF I have a soft spot for. Have I ever told you about her Joan? There are six words I think "Beauty is truth and truth beauty." That's how I think of her, but of course no words can describe her for she is unique – unique coming from the Latin and meaning "one of a kind". The only one of a kind. Here! I can't stay now writing pretty nothings. I must go to dinner.

This evening I shall write to Dad, but tonight I shall dream of you my darling.

Au revoir,
> Love from
> Len

* * *

Kimberley
26th June 1943

My Dearest Joan,
I wonder what you are doing at this moment. It's Saturday morning at 11.00hrs. I've just returned from coffee and doughnuts at the canteen. It's a long time since I've had doughnuts. Are you lucky enough to have a weekend off, or are you taking Morse? I expect by now you have reached quite a good speed. I'm still struggling with "tens" on the buzzer and "eights" on the Aldis lamp. They consider these speeds sufficient for a pilot and I'm jolly glad they do.

I was Duty Pilot on Wednesday. Nothing very much happened. I had to report a Naval Officer for bad airmanship and one of our planes was lost. Eventually the pilot phoned to say he had force landed so everything was OK.

Something amusing occurred in the mess. While waiting for the meal I read a letter from Mrs Ridsdale containing a photograph of her three children. A native waiter asked if the letter was from my wife and if she was well. On telling him I wasn't married he was most perturbed about the children. I then showed him your photograph and he was very much impressed. This particular waiter is extremely intelligent. I often have chats to him on various subjects, much to the annoyance of the South Africans.

Write soon my darling.
Always your
Len

* * *

Kimberley
4th July 1943

My Dearest Joan,
It was wonderful to hear from you again. You seem to like your new life. I'm glad Joan, and hope you will always be happy with your new-made friends. Yes dear, it was hard parting from Met. Love of man for woman is one kind of love, but love of man for man is entirely different. I was greatly attached to Met as I was to Tommy in Canada. I am still with boys I have known for two years, but I must confess I don't feel quite the same about them. However we still write to each other. At the moment there doesn't seem much chance of meeting,

but there's always the hope of being in the same aircrew. When Met has finished his course he will be a Bomb Aimer.

Which brings me back to my own marksmanship, or rather lack of it. Joan, I'm slipping badly. Remember I used to be fairly good with a rifle and at clay pigeon shooting. We've had some more shooting this past week and I hit three pigeons out of about 25. Horrible, isn't it? But worse is to follow. I was on high level bombing last week. From 10,000 ft I hit the target once. The other bombs were anything up to 100 yds away. Low level bombing at 300 ft was a little better, I hit the target three times.

So now you're an ACW2. It's a horrible feeling to receive calling up papers, isn't it. I wondered "Shall I like it?" "Shall I be homesick?" Numerous and silly questions popped from my brain. It does feel strange at first to be one of a roomful of girls (in my instance, boys of course). But I imagine all the other people feel just as shy about undressing as we do ourselves. Cold comfort!

Today I've written to the Northern Transvaal for some native carved animals and birds – to decorate a future home.

All my love,
Len x

* * *

Kimberley
4th July 1943

My Own Darling,
I was so happy to have your letter but because you are lonely I write this airgraph which should reach you much sooner than the letter. What can I say to cheer you up? I'm lonely too my dear, and long to see you again. Within a few short weeks you will be in my arms again and for a little while we can forget the world. I pray earnestly that this will be over soon. Tell me first impressions of service life. Thursday was a holiday. There were great rejoicings – one of the boys returned from hospital. Unfortunately another of my pals has been killed out here. It's one year and two days since I last saw you. Where shall we go when I come home on leave? I suppose it depends on whether or not we can get leave together. Wherever you are, I will come to see you. I love you so very much.
 Your Len

* * *

Kimberley
9th July 1943

My Dear Joan,

You seem so happy now. Are you? Service life isn't so bad after the first week or so, is it. Congratulations Joan on being able to take Morse at 6 wpm after so short a time. I can only do 10 wpm.

I'm glad you were able to tell me a little more about your inner thoughts. The possibility of a future life will be only one of many topics for us to talk about when I come home. I liked the description of your two friends. I'd like to meet Melody, who is deliciously sarcastic. I used to be told that I was sarcastic, but I'm afraid I'm not now – it's absolutely wasted on ignorant people.

Remember in my last letter I said I couldn't fire accurately with a gun anymore nor drop bombs accurately. Well, since then I won a competition for shooting and all my bombs, with the exception of one, have hit the target. I feel a little better now. Yesterday my co-pilot and I were bombing continuously for five hours with very good results.

Yes Joan, it is a year since I left England. In my last letter I said I would be coming home soon, now it appears it may be another twelve weeks or more. I wanted to be home in August to have the last of an English summer, not the beginning of winter. But I know sunshine or snow it'll be wonderful to be back among friends again. "See Naples and die." Remember that saying. I have one now. It is for me "See Joan and live." I'm only half alive now. I do feel that with you dear I could do something worthwhile.

Goodnight, Joan.
> Your loving
> Len

* * *

September 1943

My Own Darling,
I'm on my way home – to you. For me this voyage can't end soon enough. This ship, the slowest in the convoy, seems to crawl along, but however slow, we are at least going in the right direction. I thought I'd have a fairly easy time on this trip, but fate decreed otherwise. I was in charge of one of the guns for the first two days. Now myself and five pilots are on one gun. Duty is for 24 hours. Last night I slept on deck. In the early part of the night there was a moon and hundreds of stars. There was only one thing missing. Why doesn't this ship hurry, Darling. I want so much to see you again.

I intended to get one or two curios of South Africa, but we left in such a hurry none of us had a chance to get anything. I wanted to bring a small quantity of tea, sugar and butter but that wasn't possible. On the other hand I manged to get a dress length for Mum at Kimberley but on trying to get one for you I was told that material was rationed so I got something else. Consoled myself afterwards by remembering you are now in uniform so couldn't wear a dress anyway. I've managed to get some jam, condensed milk and tinned fruit on this ship for ourselves, for we both have a 21st birthday to celebrate.

Have you noticed Joan that being away, home takes on a new aspect – a new meaning. Before, in peace time, one took home more or less for granted, at least I think I did, and it's something far better than that. I'm hoping for three weeks leave so I'll be able to go home for a few days and during that time make arrangements to see you. Do you think we could have a holiday together, providing we manage to get a week's leave at the same time. In one of your letters you mentioned the "David and Joanna" story. I hope you're not looking for a literary masterpiece for really the story is quite simply written.

We crossed the equator today so at a very rough estimate we have something like 3500 miles before we reach England. Conditions on board do not improve. My only complaint is about the food. The following is the usual menu. Breakfast: porridge, unsweetened not fit to eat anyway, small pieces of bacon which the officers don't like and cold potatoes, one slice of bread and butter, jam if possible and tea which is even worse than the stuff made in South Africa. Lunch: dishwater served up as soup, stew – one spoonful, slice of bread – unsweetened custard and pudding also without sugar. All on one plate. Supper or Dinner: one or two spoonfuls of beans, one slice of bread and butter, jam if there is any left over from breakfast. Sometimes we have one slice of corned beef. My stomach aches all day from lack of food and my clothes don't fit me now. I'm fading away.

Remember me writing about a farm I wished to have after the war. It once seemed like a wonderful dream, but now I'm sure it can become a reality. I'll enlarge on this when I see you. That will not be so very long now. Three weeks at the most. What are three weeks after a whole year.

For a little while au revoir, my dearest.

Your Len

* * *

1334965
SGT. Manwaring, L.C.G.
Undated

Hullo Dear,
We are now on the last few days of the voyage and it's getting rougher every hour and very windy – so strong it's difficult to stand up in the gun turrets. I wonder where we shall go on landing. If it is to Bournemouth like last time I should be able to see you very easily. But I think we'll be sent to Harrogate – an entirely different matter. You'll be able to see from the address when I add it.

It's quite a long time since I played cards, but during this voyage I've passed many pleasant hours playing bridge. We have just sighted land – Scotland, I believe. I'm really getting too excited to write any more even to you dear. The voyage seems a thing of the distant past and South Africa just a bad dream.

Last night I tried to picture what you look like in uniform. With your new hair style I have a rough idea – slim and very smart. You always did look neat and smart whatever you were wearing. I'll finish this letter when I reach camp.

Len receiving his Wings

Len and Met in South Africa

Len, Met and Bob in South Africa

Len in South Africa

Chapter Four

Back in the U.K.

"...Perfume is unobtainable – and there are no ping-pong balls..."

September 1943 – April 1945

LEN was back in the UK and was sent to Montrose to train to be an instructor pilot. He was then stationed in Gloucestershire, near to Joan. They became engaged, and married in 1944.

"B" Squadron
Reception Wing
RAF Station
Ashville College
Harrogate
Yorkshire
9th September 1943

My Dear Joan,

Just a very hurried note telling you of my arrival back in England. Shall be on leave by Monday next, probably for two weeks. If you can get leave let me know, if not try to get a long weekend and I will come and stay with you. Can hardly believe I'm back in England once more. Have just had the best meal since I left England. Longing to see you darling. The next three days are going to be very busy here. I phoned Dad yesterday and found he was ill in bed but nothing to worry about. Excuse the short note and lack of news. I'm so excited.

    Always your
    Len

*　*　*

Margate
22nd September 1943

Joan Dear,

You've had a strange effect on me – strange for me. I seem to wander around like a lost soul. I miss you Joan. I'm so happy you loved our weekend because that means we both had a good time for I too enjoyed every minute of it. If your only possible regrets are those concerning the loss of your "standoffishness" then I don't think you need to have any regrets at all. Don't try to fight against it dear, let everything take its natural course. I've just remembered how you got your pass altered. You can tell the officer that your "fiancé" had quite a good weekend. How did your "fiancé's fiancée" enjoy it?

    Best of luck with your work.

        Always yours,

        Len

* * *

Harrogate
28th September 1943

My Dearest,

I'm back once more and my leave is just a beautiful memory. During that fourteen days I seemed to have got around quite a bit. I've been to see your Mother three times, also Gladys and Henry who came home last Wednesday for a week. Your Mother gave me your photograph – you know, the one in Uniform sitting on the wall which shows your bony knees, or so you say. Last Friday, Mum, Dad and I went to Canterbury again – stayed the night and Shirley came back with us on Saturday.

    How are you getting on and how did your tests go? My kit is here – unfortunately, for I am posted tomorrow. Where I'm going I don't know, but I'll write as soon as I get there. Sorry, must stop now and go on parade.

All my love,
Len

***

21(P) AFU
RAF Perton
The Wergs
Wolverhampton
Staffs
10th October 1943

My Dearest Joan,
I've just returned to camp and found your telegram. Thank God. But I'll tell you the awful story. Yesterday I got away from camp at 4.0pm, an hour and a half early, and was in Crewe by 7.20. I went round to the canteen (it's Church Army by the way) and not seeing you there concluded you must have gone out to get somewhere to sleep. 9 o'clock came but Joan didn't so I thought she must have missed the train, so decided to wait for the 10 o'clock. That train arrived, so did one from Preston at 3.45 in the morning. After that I decided to get a little sleep. While still thinking you might arrive at 10.00 in the morning. But when you didn't arrive I began to worry. I kept telling myself that you were alright, but horrible thoughts kept turning over in my mind. I thought you might be ill or that your pass was cancelled, but in

either of these cases I would have had a telegram. It was the lack of the telegram that did all the trouble. And then, oh darling, I shall never forget this – I thought you were dead. It's horrible to write it and I can never describe on paper how I felt. I seemed to have lost all feeling – my heart and soul wrenched from me. I wandered round in a daze – at last pulled myself together and sent off a telegram. I can see now how Fate must have laughed at me. For me it was anything but a joke. I found out just what you mean to me my dear – life itself.

I who had thought myself so cold and calm – suddenly brought face to face with the truth. I don't know why I'm telling you this – it must seem like the ramblings of a demented being but it isn't. It's just how I felt. I arrived back at camp and your telegram was in my pigeon-hole. I could have cried with relief and joy.

It's a pity your pass was cancelled. To finish this letter I'll tell you what we missed. We could have gone to a cinema show in the evening, wandered back by the light of the moon. It was a wonderful night, Joan all silver and a warm breeze blowing. In the morning the sun was shining – a nice day for a picnic. We could have taken some sandwiches and cakes out into the country for I had brought my ration bag with me. But don't worry because we missed this, there will be other times.

My darling, I must go to bed now, and loving you very much I kiss you Good Night.

Len x

***

Wolverhampton\
27 October 1943

Dearest Joan,

Your letter arrived yesterday. Yes, some of your remarks were very subtle – you naughty girl (that's coming from a naughty boy). I wonder if we will be lucky enough to see each other again on Saturday. I think I am free from 4.0pm till 23.59 on Sunday.

Saturday

JOAN

Euston	Crewe
2.40pm	6.02

LEN

Wolverhampton	Crewe
6.13pm	7.11

Sunday

JOAN

Crewe	Blackpool
7.42pm	10.03

LEN

Crewe	Wolverhampton
8.05pm	9.11

For a long time now I have thought that my flying wasn't sufficiently good to be made an instructor and I haven't bothered very much because no-one has said anything about it. For the last two days however my flying, although I say it myself, has been really good. All my landings have been "three pointers" and it's not easy to do those in these kites. I put this change down to your little chat. Thank you.

Flying was cancelled again today. We did some gardening instead. What a war! Did I tell you about the people who live in a caravan in the middle of this camp? They have a very nice caravan and a car too and about two dozen chickens. Wouldn't it be nice to have sufficient money to wander around wherever we wished to go – possibly in a caravan.

As far as I know I shall be here for another two weeks, and then going to Wheaton Ashton for four weeks. Following that, the trip up north. Wheaton Castle is 9 miles from the nearest town. What a bind.

Remember me to your Mother and Gladys.

All my love,

Len x

I am amazed how regular the train services seemed to be during the war. Also the post was delivered quickly several times a day. I presume that both these services were seen as vital to public morale. But they do not seem so efficient or reliable nowadays.

***

Wolverhampton
1 November 1943

Hello Dear,

So now you're a charming WAAF once more instead of an equally charming civilian of the past week. I've been thinking about Elsie's wedding. I guess we'll just have to go in case she throws her bouquet away. There's always a chance you might catch it – and then of course we couldn't disappoint the world, could we.

Yes, Joan it's quite in order for me to tell you about compass swinging. In theory a compass needle points always to Magnetic North (this differs by varying annual degrees from True North). But the metal structure of an aeroplane – fuselage, undercarriage, engines etc. – has a further effect on the compass needle which may cause the needle to point either to the east or west of Magnetic North. This difference is known as Deviation. In order to eliminate this deviation as much as possible, compasses are "swung" periodically. This is done by placing the aircraft (containing the compass) on the eight main headings i.e. N, NE, E, SE etc. This is done either using a master compass or on a compass marked out on the ground away from metal objects so that there is no deviation. The reading of the aircraft compass is compared with that of the master compass on these various headings and suitable tables are compiled so that the pilot will know that on a certain heading – say east – there will be a deviation of 3 degrees to the west.

All my love,
Len x

* * *

Wolverhampton
3 November 1943

Joan dear,
Today, quite by chance I glanced at the Registered Mail list and there was my name. Joan, it was a lovely surprise. A wallet is one of the things I need most and I can see I shall just have to see you next week and thank you personally. How did you get such soft leather – it's beautiful isn't it. I must keep it for special occasions. Thank you again for my 21st Birthday present. Of course I don't mind if it was belated. I'm glad you didn't send it to S.A.

Last night we went down to the Dutch Camp to see the RAF Gang Show. The show was really good. One pianoforte solo was the Warsaw Concerto which always makes me feel like crying. We now have a radiogram in our mess plus some very good records, among them the above mentioned Warsaw Concerto. Remember me telling you about a piece of music called Fingal's Cave. I heard it again yesterday.

My little WAAF Betty is on nine days compassionate leave as her mother's ill. Another WAAF here has just had news that her boyfriend has been killed and one of the fellows from here has been killed on his first op. All the bad news seems to arrive at once.

This enforced inactivity is boring.

Always yours,
Len

* * *

Wolverhampton
8 November 1943

My Dearest Joan,

I still have Saturday off so I will see you at about 7.15 at the CA Canteen, Crewe. I'm so glad you are coming. You'll probably arrive before me so do you think you could have a bun and some tea if you are hungry, then we could go to the pictures straight away. After that we'll – no I'll keep that as a surprise, then we'll go to the hotel. I think we'll be in bed long before midnight. Does that suit you Madam?

I'm going to tell the boss this afternoon that I'm going to see my young lady and ask her to become my fiancée. Then another time I'll have to try for a 48 in order to meet my young lady and get a ring.

Last Friday night I went to the Dutch camp with one of the boys and gambled. I came back with 3/- to the good. On Saturday I did some shopping in town. Bought a present for Elsie and Reg and sent it off. In the afternoon I went to the pictures in camp – "Comrades Strike at Dawn". It was very good. Have you seen it?

I'll say au revoir now. So get your pass in and I'll see you on Saturday.

Always yours,
Len

* * *

Wolverhampton
10 November 1943

Hullo Joan,

Just after I'd sealed the last envelope I was told I could have Sunday off. My prayer was answered very quickly. It seems that our luck has changed at last, doesn't it. There will be a full moon on Friday. It will be two months since we met in London – remember there was a moon then. Oh, I almost forgot to tell you. I've written to the Royal Hotel and asked them for bed and breakfast and I sent a deposit.

The woods here look beautiful now. The ferns are nearly all brown – just here and there are a few green ones. The trees are covered with red and brown leaves.

You'd have a lovely time stamping on all the leaves as you walked through the paths. At night too it's lovely. I noticed last night as I rode through the moon made everything silver, there was just a slight mist.

Au revoir, my darling. Only three days now.

All my love,

Len

* * *

Sgts Mess
RAF Station
Little Ann
Church Eaton
Staffs
30th November 1943

Hullo Dear,

So glad you got to your billet alright. For a long time I couldn't make out what you meant by saying vests came in useful sometimes. Then I remembered you telling me you didn't wear them (as though I didn't know). I'm so happy you loved our weekend. I did too dear, and as for the rest of what you said, there's only one thing to do – see each other again.

I did one flip this afternoon. Weather is very bad. I took my first WAAF for a ride too. She just sat in the kite while I taxied it in for a major inspection.

I wrote to Uncle John today and told him about "my love". He had asked if I had a young lady and hoped that I would find a suitable partner and that we would have a happy union. I had previously told him about Elsie getting married. As I wrote about you so I lived the past five years again. I didn't think I knew so much about you. It was wonderful. In the future I shall look back on our weekend as one of the happiest times of my life. I can't write more now, my heart is so full.

Goodnight dearest,
Len x

* * *

Church Eaton
1 December 1943

Joan dear,
You've made me so very happy. I, too, feel as though I'm in another world. This feeling of love and beauty seems unreal on this war-shattered earth. I've flown high above the clouds where the earth can't be seen. That's in another world too. Whenever we're together, even though it may only be for a few hours, we can build our castles and be happy planning for the future. It's going to be a wonderful future, isn't it.

How I'll love telling you all sorts of stories – about how the young native keeps himself warm while guarding his cattle by lighting a fire in an ant hill – or about the native dancing and singing – or even about the native wars. Because of the war I suppose we are forced to look upon the dark side for a while, but let us not dwell too long. Yes dear, life is swift and uncertain, but our love will keep us together. Don't you believe that too? This war has taken a more personal tone, because it is keeping us from being together. Is it wrong to think like that? I wish it was all over.

God bless you and keep you safe till we meet again.
Your own
Len

* * *

Church Eaton
4 December 1943

My Dearest Joan,
I'm so happy to have another letter from you today, just to keep me going over the weekend. We didn't fly yesterday as the weather was so bad. It was very cold too and we had nothing to light a fire with. (Never end a sentence with a preposition – I know!) So we went on the scrounge, first to get paper. DROs, time sheets and similar documents came in very handy. The big boss supplied coke, though he didn't know it. We "bor-

rowed" a packing case for wood and then pinched some oil to make things complete and get a good fire going.

I wrote to your mother on Thursday but I didn't say anything about our becoming engaged yet. I told Mum and Dad over the phone on Thursday evening that we thought of becoming engaged. So there's no need to postpone indefinitely as you suggest. I miss you so very much dearest.

Au revoir now, Joan. I have some work to do.

All my love

Len x

* * *

Church Eaton
12 December 1943

Hullo dear,

I'm back in camp once more. I looked for a letter from you – and I was lucky. There were two returned from South Africa before you were posted to Blackpool.

I'll give you a detailed account of the wedding. It was beautiful. Bert and I slept in a house a few doors away on Friday night. The bedroom was exactly how I'd like to have one. The room had light coloured paper with very pretty corner pieces. Just above the bed, which was very comfortable (I can't stand feather beds, can you?) was a lamp. Another light hung down by the bay window where was the dressing table – a very modern affair with neat drawers and a triple mirror.

The day of the Great Event came. Elsie almost had a completely white wedding for it started to snow in the morning. However in the afternoon it was very sunny and a little chilly. While waiting for the Bride to come I read the marriage ceremony in the Prayer Book. It's rather frightening. Have you read it? It was a choral wedding. The choir preceded the Bride up to the chancel steps. The first hymn was "Lead us Heavenly Father, lead us." I found myself strangely affected by the service. Why I don't know. Maybe I was imagining myself before the altar saying "I will". It's a simple service, Joan, but it's sacred and beautiful. I'm glad you don't want to be married at a registry office.

The service lasted about half an hour and after the photographs had been taken outside the church, we all went to a nearby house for the reception. The room was beautifully laid out. Little fairy lights all over the room provided the lighting. Shall I dare to tell you what we ate? OK I will then. Cold meat and salad followed by jelly etc. Then beer or soft drinks. Later on when the cake was cut we had wine for the toasts. The meal finished, the room was cleared and there was dancing until 7.30 when we returned to Grange Road and continued the merry making. Everyone was happy. Mum even got up once and did the Lambeth Walk. If you had been there you could have blushed with me when I was asked when the next wedding would be. Rather a tall order when I'm not even engaged yet.

Goodnight my love,

Len x

(x) This is for the morning

* * *

Church Eaton
18 December 1943

My Own Darling,

Thank you for your letter and also your parcel. I thought I'd better let you know it's safe and I'll try hard not to open it till 25th. Don't you think I could have just a little peep now. You've certainly been lucky with your presents so far. I had a parcel from Auntie Dolly containing all sorts of useful things, stationery, razor blades, shaving soap, a diary and some stamps.

I'm waiting for your Mother to reply. Do you think she's turned me down? Mum and Dad sent their love in a letter today and hoped we'd be very happy. We will, won't we. Charles and I went to the station cinema last night. It was a very good show called "Silver Fleet" dealing with the underground movement in Holland. It was a true story. I'd love to do exciting things like they did, steal submarines, blow up ammunition dumps, oil storage tanks and other things. However maybe I'll feel a little better later as we are flying tonight.

I was going to tell you about Uncle Harry in Wales. He's a foreman on one of the mines. I think he's an engineer who maintains surface equipment. He's converted his cottage into quite a modern place. Two rooms have been added and also a bathroom. The marvellous part of it all is that he's done it himself. Last year he made a greenhouse – the material cost £120, but in this year he has made £90 in tomatoes alone. I just mentioned that to show that a living can be made. Next time we meet we must certainly discuss the farm. If we both agree about it then I don't see what can stop us. Don't worry about the rabbits, Joan. I'm not keen on them myself. And in any case they would definitely be as far from the house as possible – likewise the chickens. I think I'd like to have a tennis court with our house. I liked your finishing touches to the bedroom I mentioned. I always knew you had good taste.

Your loving
Len x

In 1948, Joan and Len moved into a council house in Margate and they did keep some livestock. I remember two chickens called Arabella and Bertha who produced eggs. There were also two rabbits, Ping and Pong. I still have the scar on my finger when one of them bit me.

Ten years later, after a couple of moves, they bought a plot of land in Wallingford, Berkshire and Len designed their bungalow.

* * *

Church Eaton
20 December 1943

My Dearest Love,

Christmas has always been a time for family reunions, hasn't it. Tough we can't be home together. I'm glad I'm in England for this Christmas. Let us hope and pray that we shall be together next year.

Today I received <u>the</u> letter from your Mother. Everything's alright. Oh Joan, it's such a nice letter. Your Mother writes *"may she be as dear to you as she has been to me always"*. I think you know the answer to that, don't you dear. So now we have good wishes for our future happiness from your Mother and from my Mum and Dad. There's no need to wait any longer than necessary. I wonder if Fate will be kind to us and we have leave together. Joking apart, I do wish we could know definitely. We are becoming engaged, aren't we, in January and we will be married a few months later. We'll be so happy together and what fun we'll have. I've been dreaming of the time when we'll have our own home – having our meals together – going to a show in the evening or sitting quietly by the fire. It's going to be wonderful Joan, isn't it.

    Your very own
        Len who loves you very much
        xxxxxxxxxxxx

* * *

Church Eaton
22 December 1943

Dearest Joan,
I'm thinking about you and feel rather lost and wish that I could be with you. How did the party go – and more important, how about the exams. Did you have any sticky questions or was it a piece of cake. When I finished flying last night I had a lovely roast dinner followed by jam tart and custard.

    Official secrets – since we started night flying we've had quite a number of accidents – two serious ones. One aircraft was completely burnt out – on another occasion one of the pilots walked into a prop, but he's practically OK. Last night your little Lennie nearly got into trouble. One of my engines cut out as I was taking off – I corrected for it and then it picked up again. Later on the brakes failed. Am I lucky! Everything's OK.

    It's to bed now, so Goodnight my love.
        All my love,

Len xx
Happy Christmas

* * *

26 December 1943

My Dearest Joan,

Christmas is over now. How did you enjoy yourself? On Christmas Eve we cycled down to a public house called the Swan. By "we" I mean Charles, two other fellows, Chris and Johnny, and myself. We had a couple of drinks and then a lovely pork chop. I can't ever remember having a chop which tasted as good as that. We cycled back to camp, stopping on the way to sing a carol outside a farmhouse. Back at camp we talked about what we were doing at Christmas last year. Christmas 1942, John, Chris and I were on the *Letitia* arriving in England.

The only reason I got up early Christmas Day was to have my egg for breakfast. It was worth getting up for. The dinner was the best I've seen. Turkey, ham, baked potatoes, sprouts etc., followed by Christmas pudding and then cigarettes. In the afternoon Charles, Chris and myself went out for a walk. We put on our *"boots, rubber knee airmen for the use of"* as it was muddy and we just tramped all over the fields and through the woods hardly walking on the roads at all. It was great. I must admit we were rather like young children but we thoroughly enjoyed ourselves, so why worry!

Since Christmas morning I've been carrying your wallet and photograph with me. Joan darling – I love it – thank you dear. I'm going to tell you a secret. You know that letter you wrote a few weeks ago – in fact <u>the</u> letter when you told me you loved me whatever may happen, I've been carrying it in my battledress pocket ever since. Now it is with your photograph in my new wallet. It's such a beautiful letter and I think you know how much it means to me.

Bags of panic in the Crew Room now so maybe I'd better say "Goodnight Sweetheart". I wish I could say "See you in the morning."

Goodnight my love,
Len x

I have <u>the</u> letter. It was still in the envelope inside Len's wallet. It was written in green ink. The photograph was there too.

* * *

4845277 ACW2 FILMER J
c/o Mrs Metcalfe
30 Hornby Road
Blackpool
Lancs
29 November 1943

Dearest,

I don't know why I'm writing. I've nothing particular to say. I'm still dreamy about our weekend. It's still too near to have become a memory. I feel so much more at ease with you than I ever did before. I want long hours with you – in easy chairs or laying in the grass under the sun and for you to talk to me, to tell me about Africa, all the things one wants to know about a strange country and a strange people. And for you to tell me all the things you did and the things you thought. We've had no time to get to know each other again mentally, have we? My opinions have changed – broadened on many things as yours must have – but one can't afford to talk desultorily when the last four hours are flying by.

Life is swift – and uncertain in our time – we can but plan, hoping that our plans will become reality. Whatever happens I want you to know I love you. How often I've said I never wanted to fall in love – how often I've said I'd never get married.

I feel very happy tonight, there is something so uplifting – for lack of a better word – in loving and being loved. Do you feel that? It depends I know on what kind of mood you are in, how you receive this letter. You will probably take it facetiously – and wonder what on earth is wrong with me. Don't answer this – let me imagine your mood falls in with mine and you read into every word the meaning it was written with.

Goodnight my dear – it seems right to say, God keep you.
    All my love,
    Your Joan

* * *

Church Eaton
1st January 1944

Hullo dear,

Congratulations on passing your exams – also to Ann. I'm so sorry about Melody, but don't give up hope. You may still be together sometime. Yes, it is nice of Elsie to offer to lend you her wedding dress and veil.

You wanted to know more about the chicken farm. I've got all the gen concerning initial costs and profit which begins about three months after we start. It's the first day of the New Year. Let us hope it will be a happy one for us. Our Year, in fact.

All my love,
Len xxxxxx

* * *

Church Eaton
11th January 1944

My Dearest,

I'm going to make you envious. We've had a fire in our hut continuously for two days now. It's lovely. We are now getting much better meals again. I'm always thinking of my stomach, aren't I?

Now to the subject of the second page of your letter – sex and marriage. It's rather a new thing for you to write about, but as you say we must face facts. From what little you've told me regarding your views on sex I don't think we'll have any trouble adjusting ourselves because our views are similar. I don't like the idea of you gaining all this knowledge when I can't have it as well. Maybe you'd better bring the books along with you when we meet. Quite frankly dear, I may have appeared to have some knowledge of sexual matters, but what little I know I read in that 9^{d} book for the forces and from listening to fellows in the hut which is rather sordid. I'm friendly with a married fellow so maybe I'll ask him a few things, though I intend to ask Dad when I go home on leave.

Met has passed out and is now a Bomb Aimer. He's staying in SA as an instructor for now. Write soon darling.

All my love,
Len xxx

* * *

Little Ann
19th January 1944

My Own Darling,
This is your birthday letter and with it I sent my sincerest wishes, my love, and my hopes that we will be together very soon. I love the way you speak about our future home – and children. Yes Joan, I do like the idea of a

polished table and I too had thought of candles but in a rather different way. I thought it would be nice to celebrate anniversaries of birthdays and our wedding day by having dinner. Just the two of us with lighted candles on the table, and as you say a nice fire to sit by afterwards.

I often visualise little parts of our married life as I hope they will be. It does seem such a long time ahead though that one is apt to regard it as more of a fairy tale than a possible reality. We will have those things. We'll have to wait and work, but half the fun and pleasure will be in striving to achieve our goals.

Have you noticed the "tripe" being written in the press lately about the boys conscripted to work in the mines. "Bevan boys like work down in the pits" and such like. Can you imagine any soldier enjoying his first few days in the army? All this talk about pit boys seems to be rather stupid.

About this cooking business. It's a jolly poor show, but I guess you'll do. After all, I can always go out for meals or alternatively I could have a camp fire in the garden and cook my own. And as for getting to a man's heart through his stomach I think this case is different for you've wriggled your way there already. What am I writing all this nonsense for when I know that you are or will be quite capable of cooking nice meals. Anyway I'd still love you even if you couldn't cook.

I've had a gentle hint from Mum that our garden needs digging over. I must do that when I go home. In about an hour I'll be able to eat again. I seem to eat an awful lot, but I don't get any fatter – thank goodness. Oh darling, I want to see you so much.

Good night Beloved, God bless you.

All my love,

Len xxxxxxxxxxxxxxxxxxxxxxxxxxxxx

* * *

Little Ann
Staffs
26th January 1944

My Dearest,

I can't help thinking how heavenly it will be when we are married. Just imagine – we won't have to say goodbye, just goodnight and then go to sleep. And then in the morning – you'll be the first person I see. Remember at Crewe we talked about children and you said you wanted an anaesthetic when you have our children? Yesterday I read an article in *Reader's Digest* about this. It appears that you can have a baby without any pain or discomfort. But of course there has to be a snag. The operation has to be performed by a highly skilled surgeon. It is known as "continuous caudal analgesia". I'm not sure whether it's practical in England as yet, but it's successful in America.

Aren't these engagement cards nice. I've had one from Mum and Dad and one from Mother and Gladys. With all these kind thoughts pouring in we can't be anything but happy. I've deposited another £5 in the Post Office, so we now have £20 in there towards that beautiful ring you'll be wearing soon. No more news for now. I love you Joan.

 All my love,
 Len xx

* * *

Little Ann
Staffs
31st January 1944

Joan darling,
Would you like our engagement announced in the local press or would you prefer to wait till you have the ring. I hope that won't be too long now.

Had some fun this afternoon. I climbed up (in a kite of course) right through the clouds and flew along about 200ft above them. After a while I noticed another aircraft a little behind on my starboard side. It turned out to be one of the boys so we did a spot of formation flying, then he gave the magic signal and we broke away and zoomed among the clouds and did a spot of dog fighting. Oh boy it was good. It's ages since I've had a trip like that. Wish you had been there with me.

Best of luck to you and your pals for the exams in the near future.

All my love,
Len xx

* * *

Little Ann
Staffs
1st February 1944

My Darling,
I'm on my way home on leave. I haven't told you about my new job after the war. It's a wizard idea. Cycling back from Stafford some time ago Bill and I stopped on the canal bridge and watched the barges go by. These are long narrow barges – some self-propelled – some horse drawn with a tow rope. They have a stove on board and at the blunt end there appears to be sufficient room for a bedroom. Anyway, most of the barges seem to have a family on board. I wonder what life would be like sailing along the canals of England, picking up one cargo here and another load somewhere else. No – perhaps it wouldn't be too good – a little monotonous.

2nd February

At home. I arrived about 8 o'clock last night, had a nice fish supper and played records on the gramophone. Then I went to see your Mother and Gladys. While I was there Henry came home for 48 hrs. My Mum was saying that we had some furniture to start a home but then she went on "I don't think Joan likes sleeping with anyone does she, so maybe you'd better look out for some twin beds." To which I smiled inwardly and answered "I don't know, Mum, but I'm also used to sleeping alone, but I suppose we can get used to sleeping together." Isn't it fun!

I have a plan for 16th February. We could travel down separately and spend the night in London and then catch an early train (Victoria 8.35) and arrive in Margate in time to get your engagement ring before lunch. We can then have a party and share out the pineapple and jam. I imagine with a little persuasion we could get Mum and Gladys to bed and make ourselves comfortable on the settee.

Snags? If I can't get off at all, you could get the ring yourself at Margate. I've made arrangements with Dad about the money. He will give you a check and I'll pay him when I come home. It's nice of him, but it doesn't seem right. I'd like to go into the shop, get the ring, hand over the cash and then put the ring on your finger. Oh darling, I'm miserable without you. Here's hoping and praying we will be able to see each other on 16th.

Au revoir dearest,
Your loving
Len xxxx

* * *

Little Ann
Staffs
8th February 1944

Hello Darling,
The worst – or almost the worst has happened. My 48 hours extension was granted but on Monday I was recalled immediately by telegram pending a posting today. I hoped I might be posted nearby so I could still see you on Sunday. Darling, here's the news. I'm off to Scotland tonight – to Montrose. Looks as though you're never to get that ring. Would you like to get the ring yourself? Mum will come with you and Dad will give you a cheque. Get the ring you like and I'll give Dad the money back later on. I'll write as soon as I reach Montrose. Good luck dear.
Your loving Len xxxx

* * *

Sgts Mess
RAF Station
Montrose

Angus
Scotland
11th February 1944

My Own Darling,
We arrived in camp about 5.30pm just in time for tea. I'm billeted in what used to be the Married Quarters. These are five-roomed houses and quite comfortable. There is one other fellow in the room with me. We have a nice fire in the corner of the room. I've just had lunch – steak, which was nicely cooked. The breakfasts are not very good but the rest of the meals are quite OK. Yesterday morning I woke up to find snow all over the country but by lunchtime the sun had melted practically all the snow. It's not so cold up here as I had been led to believe. But dear me, it's miles from home.

I found out from Pay Accounts yesterday that when we are married I pay 10/6 a week income tax instead of 17/6. I shall be able to save at least £2 a week. I actually receive £3.4 a week. Well 4/- will go in stamps, soap and odd bits and pieces. I'll try to save the other pound for leave. I estimate that our wedding including honeymoon, your dresses etc. will cost £100. I can save £50 by the end of July. I spoke to your Mother and my Mum and Dad and they have no objection to us getting married during the war. My darling, I love you more and more each day.

I have a 48hr pass in about four weeks so I shall go down to see Tommy at Leuchars. Haven't seen him since 1941.

Au revoir, dearest.
All my love,
Len xxxxx

* * *

Montrose
Scotland
14th February 1944

My Darling,
Your letter today cheered me up no end. So I've about got over the shock of being posted up here and resigned to the utter disappointment I felt at not being able to see you. Did I tell you that Montrose is right on the coast. Inland about 30 miles are the hills and mountains with snow on them, making a very picturesque scene especially when the sun is shining. We have to wear Mae Wests as well as parachutes here because some of the flying is done over water.

Before I go any further, congratulations Joan, darling, on getting your sparks. But then I felt sure you would. I'm proud of you dear. I suppose you know you've passed the hardest course in the RAF and I gather it's the worst bird of the lot.

I had to interrupt this letter and do a trip. Guess I must be dead lucky 'cos I tipped the kite right up on its nose, buried the undercarriage and part of the props in the ground and got out quite safely. This happened at our auxiliary 'drome. Thought I might have stayed there all night, but one of the boys came out for me. Wish I'd had my camera with me. It was a funny sight to see the kite sitting with the tail right up in the air. Of course I had to make a report out about it and see the boss. Everything's OK and I'm not being charged. There was practically no evidence anyway.

You'll be on leave now and I hope having that well-earned rest and playing the gramophone. Au revoir for now.

>Your ever loving
>Len xx

* * *

>Montrose
>Scotland
>23rd February 1944

My Dearest Joan,
I'm glad you've got the ring and happier still to know that you like it. I can always say "Well dear, you chose it." The design is rather unusual but I might have expected your choice would be out of the ordinary – as

unique as possible. Mum and Dad have both written to say how nice it is.

The next thing we've got to do is to decide about the wedding date. This of course depends on various factors. I suppose you still want to marry me. Yes, I was afraid of that. Seriously Joan, I think it should be the end of July or the beginning of August. (Rather exciting to think how near we are to those months. I still can't believe it's us I'm writing about. I believe you said in your letter "it seems unreal.")

Have you got anywhere in mind for our honeymoon? I've thought of five districts of the British Isles: The West Country, North Wales, The Lake District, Scotland, The Isle of Man. Would you like to stay at a hotel, or a farm house, in the country or by the sea.

Goodnight my own darling.

All my love,

Len xxx

The engagement ring that Joan chose was rectangular with an emerald in one corner and radiating rows of diamonds, set in platinum. It suited her long slender fingers well. My Mum bequeathed all her jewellery to me and I wear many of her necklaces regularly. But my fingers are short so I knew I would never wear her engagement ring. I eventually gave it back to my Dad so that he could give it to Elizabeth five years after their wedding. She loves it and wears it. I think my Mum would have approved.

* * *

Montrose
7th March 1944

My Dearest Joan,

Write and ask Elsie if you can borrow her wedding dress. Or I may be able to get some coupons from my Auntie Nell. I suppose a nightie is almost as important to you as the wedding dress. Won't you need a costume as well.

I went to Edinburgh last week and stayed with Tommy at his house. I had a wonderful time there. His sister and mother are just grand. We went sightseeing in the morning and the snow was quite deep, but it was lovely. Mum and Dad came up here for their honeymoon. It's certainly a nice place to come to. My native curios have arrived from South Africa – an elephant and two birds made from animal horn. Mum says they're wonderful.

I think I've been away from you too long now. It's about six weeks. I shall have forgotten what you look like soon. I shall be having leave from 27th April for a week but not before that date.

Au revoir,
    Your loving
    Len

I remember the birds carved from horn. They sat in front of the windows on either side of the fireplace. There was also a wooden box from South Africa which had sliding panels that had to be pushed in a specific order to open it. It intrigued me as a child.

* * *

Montrose
Scotland
22nd March 1944

Joan My Dearest,
Last night I finished reading the book on contraception. Well it's certainly set out in detail. I don't wonder you described it as cold-blooded. There are quite a number of questions I'd like to ask you, but I hardly like to ask them in a letter. There'll be plenty of time when we meet. I suppose you've heard about the ban on the South Coast again. This will probably mean we will not be able to have many people down for our wedding.

In the *Mirror* this week they are giving Spring fashions and how to make them from last year's efforts. Jane is now in the Black Market only she doesn't know it. Garth has landed in another country and Zola has knocked out some fellow with her foot.

Your very own Len x

Jane, Garth and Zola were popular cartoon characters in daily comic strips which appeared in the *Daily Mirror*. Jane boosted morale during the war as her escapades frequently led to her losing her clothes to reveal her lacy underwear. Somehow she was perceived as saucy rather than salacious.

* * *

Montrose
30th March 1944

My Dearest Joan,

I'm feeling very happy to day. Maybe it's the Spring – maybe it's because I had your letter. I'm very well, thank you darling, and we're having lovely weather here too.

Mum says the wedding dress has arrived complete with slip and veil. She says it will not need much alteration to fit you. She's put it in a suitcase together with my curios and takes it down the dug-out whenever she has to go down. You know they must be having a terrible time there, but Mum always writes cheerful letters.

<u>POST SCRIPT</u> Did I say the weather was nice here. It's just started to rain – sorry, snow, and I wanted to go down town. I'm not afraid of a little snow – I'm going down town.

    Au revoir, my Dearest.
    Your loving Len xxx

We often ask people what they would save first if their house was on fire, and nowadays the answer is often the mobile phone. So I was fascinated to know about my Nan's reaction during the air raids; her house might be bombed but my Mum's wedding dress would be safe!

* * *

> Montrose
> Scotland
> 12th April 1944

Joan dearest,
Yes dear, I had heard about your leave being stopped, and it made me mad. I felt like breaking all the windows in the camp. I think the ban will be on till June. The best thing I can suggest is for you to see the officer in charge of your section. Tell him or her what the position is regarding leave – it's important for trying on your dress, Banns etc. If you get no satisfaction, then see the C.O.

I guess you've had your cosmetics. Montrose is out of them. I did get two small jars of vanishing cream. They are not the popular brand so that's why I only got small ones – perfume is unobtainable – and there are no ping pong balls. Sorry dear – you'll have to be naturally beautiful. I could get some perfume by making love to a WAAF here and possibly some Ponds vanishing cream. Do you think it's worth it?

Mum asked me if I thought you'd like a tea service and if so what colour. I'd prefer to choose our own. It's going to be fun wandering round the shops. I've got lots to do now and I'm flying again tonight so I'll say au revoir.

    Your own
    Len x

* * *

Montrose
24th April 1944

My Own Darling,
Once again with censorship in force one doesn't feel like writing normal letters, especially when the letters are censored by officers who are my pals. It takes the personal touch away from a letter. But it will be different when I am on leave and I can write what I feel.

I had a letter from Met today. He sends you his very best wishes and says he's sorry he'll not be home in time for the Great Day. I haven't heard from Charles since I wrote weeks ago. You mention POW letters. Eventually I sent mine to George and this time it wasn't returned. One might almost say it's scandalous the way things are banned now. I don't mind [*section cut out of letter*] I do think that POWs should still have their mail.

Only another four hours and I'll be on the train going south. Think I'll have to come up here again some day for a holiday. I like it here. Would you be interested in some Max Factor powder, colour: ochre, and if you're a very good girl I'll get some table tennis balls from home.

Keep smiling dear.

All my love,

Len x

I can read Morse. Thank you for your message. I do too – only you not me.

J. Warwick [*censor*]

George, Joan's oldest brother, was in the army and was a prisoner of war in Germany.

* * *

Margate
26th April 1944

My Own Darling,

I almost put Home as the address. It does feel so good to be here. Wait till I tell you the good news then you'll be happy too. Well darling, I tried to get posted as near as possible to you and the C.O. said he couldn't do any better than post me to South Cerney. What do you say to that. The news almost left me speechless. It seems almost too good to be true but I've got it down in black and white on my pass, warrant card and route form. After all this time we'll be together.

Shall I bring the wedding dress with me for you to try on. Shall I bring the clothing coupons from your Mother so that we can get some of your things in one of the towns down west, Bristol, Gloucester etc.

It's grand to be home again. I've never looked forward to a leave so much – and next week we'll be together

All my love,
Len xx

* * *

Margate
27th April 1944

My Own Darling,
Yesterday I went to Parrotts and decided on a wedding invitation card – 50 for 18/6 including envelopes. As soon as we know the time and date we can have them printed. I haven't definitely ordered them in case we see some nicer ones in Cirencester. I made enquiries at the Police Station. It appears that the ban on the coastal belt is purely a military affair. All I have to do is get permission from my adjutant and I can have as many people here as I like. Seems strange, but as soon as I arrive I'll go and flannel the adj.

I went to see the vicar. He's an extremely nice fellow. We got chatting about all sorts of things. I gave him all the particulars he required about us. He will read the Banns for the first time this Sunday. They last for a year and it is not necessary for them to be read in Cirencester. However if we can't manage to get home we can be married down there. We've had another wedding present – from Mr Scarlett, Dad's governor. It's a gateleg table with semi-circular folding ends – dark oak.

Do you really think I'm a big wangler – well maybe I am. I kept a copy of the letter I wrote to the C.O. so I could show you. I said I wanted to be considered for posting to South Cerney as my future wife was now stationed there. "Look here old boy, do this or else." He had no option, did he. What a marvellous thought it was when I wrote "my future wife." It won't be long now before I can write "my wife."

Although we're going to be at the same camp, it's been a long time since we met. I was wondering if I'd be shy – and if you would. I want you so much my love. And of course you can sleep in my arms. We'll certainly have that flip together now. You can take off and I'll do the landing.

Your very own
Len xxx

To: C.I, No 2 F.I.S. MONTROSE
FROM: 1334965 SGT MANWARING, L.C.G.
DATE: 8th APRIL 1944

Sir,

I have the honour to request that I may be considered for posting to No 3 (P) A.F.U. SOUTH CERNEY for domestic reasons.

The reason for this request is that I am to be married within three months – sometime in July – and my future wife is now stationed at South Cerney.

I have the honour to be,

Sir,

Your obedient servant

Leonard C. G. Manwaring, SGT

* * *

Block 47
RAF South Cerney
Cirencester
Glos
18th May 1944

My Dear Joan,

For a long time last night I wrestled with my thoughts and feelings. I believed I loved you as I always have. It seemed impossible that anything could change that. I deliberately brought before me all sorts of obstacles which might have prevented me from loving you – all sorts of little things which you had said and which I had said too. Small insignificant things in themselves, yet put together they seemed horrible thoughts like towering giants in our path.

Believe this Joan: Last night when you first asked me to go to the dance I said no – I didn't feel like going. In the cinema I was overcome with such a wonderful feeling of love for you – I wanted to go to the dance – I really did want to go just to be with you and because you wanted me to. Then of course as you know I had my battledress on – I couldn't very well dance in that. Then you said you didn't want to disappoint Maurice (one of the small insignificant things). Then again in the dance I asked if you'd come out – but no you wouldn't do this for me. Then it seemed that you could dance with anyone else, but were tired when dancing with me. It hurts me when I see you surrounded with so many fellows. I'm not grumbling now dear – I'm just trying to give you my point of view.

And then the most horrible thing happened. I find it difficult to believe that I made you unhappy. The one thing I want to do is to make you happy and to share that happiness with you. My only excuse is pride I guess, but with you dearest I want to bury my pride. How could I ever make the woman I love deliberately unhappy – and I do love you Joan. Believe that. I know that to be true now. I love you as I hoped I would and as I knew I did deep down in my heart.

Last night you said there was nothing to forgive – that it was all your fault. That's not so. Maybe we were both to blame but I shouldn't have been so horrible.

These things seem to have been piling up ever since I came here. I guess last night was about the climax. You have your troubles and worries too dear, but you can do something about them, I can't. I just have to sit and wait and hope that they'll pass over quickly. I think possibly that's the whole reason for this unpleasantness.

How glad I am it's over now. We can be happy again together. I'm not going away for my 48. In fact I've told the Flight Commander it's no longer necessary, but thanked him very much for arranging it. I don't feel that I can go away until I've seen you again. If you feel as I do now, everything will be alright – because now I don't believe I love you, I know I do. I love you Joan oh so much. I'll see you sometime on Friday. We'll do as you said last night – we'll start again. I don't think we'll find it hard. We love each other – that should be sufficient for anything. It will be in the future.

I'm waiting for you dearest,
    With all my love,
    Len xx

They obviously made up after their quarrel as they were married in Margate on 29th July 1944. It must have been sad for

Joan to have the wedding without her brothers. Joan and Len had a short honeymoon in Reading before returning to South Cerney.

* * *

South Cerney
15th August 1944

My Dearest,
This evening I wanted so much to take you in my arms and kiss you, but it didn't seem right with the others there. I send you my kisses and my love. They are with you tonight and always.

How disappointed you must feel about this posting. For myself I shall say nothing except that if you go you will take part of me with you. We've got out of one posting already. What we've done once we can do again. Don't give up hope my love. You have the Padre to go to. Tell him or maybe say that little prayer of your again "Please God, let me stay." Lay it on the line – thick and heavy.

Till tomorrow, au revoir.
    All my love sweetheart,
    Len xxxx

Joan's posting was cancelled and she remained at South Cerney with Len. For these months there were very few letters as they saw each other regularly. But I did find a few scrappy undated notes like this:

Dearest Joan,
We are finishing at 1.0 o'clock tomorrow so I'll be able to see you at 5.0 o'clock outside the gates
    Cheerio till then.
        All my love,
        Len x

From *Brylcreem and Black Ties*
There were no married quarters for newlyweds at South Cerney but we managed to get the occasional weekend away to visit the wonderful villages in the Cotswolds that seemed to be untouched by the war. We did silly things like buying a set of Pyrex dishes and a rolling pin even though we had no home to go to. Sadly Joan died just two years short of our 60th wedding anniversary but I still use that rolling pin to make pastry.

* * *

"A" Sqdn 1 Flt
Sgts Mess
RAF Whitley Bay
Northumberland
16th February 1945

My Darling Joan,

I've been so lucky the last two days – I had two letters and a parcel. You're a naughty girl to send me your rations but you're a darling. I received a Valentine card from a girlfriend. Of course I don't know who she is although the card came from Cirencester and was posted exactly the same time as your letter! It's the first Valentine I've ever had.

A couple of days ago I was in charge of my Squadron. We each have to do this in turn, but when it was my turn we had to be on Colour Hoisting Parade. So Joe (that's me) not only had to lead my Sqd, but all the other Sqds in the unit.

And now once more I must bid you goodnight. What about that Valentine? If you sent it I love it and you, if you didn't then I just love you.

Goodnight, my love.

Your ever loving husband,
Len xxxx

* * *

Whitley Bay
18th February 1945

My Dearest Joan,
The whole weekend has been messed up because of a stupid church parade today which lasted thirty minutes.

However the meals were a lot better today. We had a real egg for breakfast.

The course is proving to be more interesting as time passes. We do a small amount of P/T and swimming. Likewise a small amount of actual drill. Rifle and bayonette drill figure fairly prominently. We are also taught how to remove mines and clear a way through a mine field. Also field engineering which includes ropes and rope climbing, knots, improvisation of all sorts of things in the field, bridge building, cooking. One thing I almost forgot – unarmed combat – oh and another – first aid and prevention of disease. Tomorrow we are out on a night exercise. We have to defend a vital point while the other two squadrons attack. It's going to be quite a realistic affair, even using blank ammo. I must admit I rather enjoy looking like a soldier – possibly because it's scruffy and you know I just love it when I can look scruffy.

Nothing more to write this time. Au revoir, my love. Write soon.

>All my love,
>Len
>I give you as always your goodnight kiss. xxxx

* * *

Whitley Bay
28th February 1945

Hullo Darling,

Only one more week and then we'll be together again. I think this last week will prove to be the worst as far as this course is concerned. We've got to go out on the range again, do an assault course, and then stay out for a day with only a couple of sandwiches.

I was going to tell you about the night exercise. Two squadrons were S.S. troops defending a submarine yard and vital factory. I was in this crowd and in charge of a section. The remaining squadron was divided into British units of Commandos, Airborne Troops and Marines. We, the Nazis, lost the battle, but I'm rather pleased because my section was the only one to arrive back at the factory almost intact – we came up behind the British troops and picked them off one by one. Afterwards we learned from the umpires that we had inflicted most of the casualties.

Myself and my second in command went along our lines checking up to see if the men were OK. At one place they were all chatting away in a bunch. I told them to get back to their posts – not forgetting my Heil Hitler. Then we decided to come back a different way and surprise them. As we were crawling along a ditch, we saw the enemy about 100 yds away making straight for our lines. So we started back, then we were crawling along one side of a hedge and the enemy were crawling along on the other side. We met at a break in the hedge and were awarded two casualties. Then we continued to our lines – likewise the enemy and our boys were really awake – they got the whole bunch of commandos. At the end of the exercise I had a flash bomb left and let it off while everyone was nattering. Most unpopular!

Remember me telling you about those improvised cooking stoves and kitchens? Well we've had our meals cooked on them twice this week out on the range – and the meals are better than in the mess.

Joan, you really are a naughty girl going home without permission. I hope you're right about the consequences being over by the time I get back. They probably will be if you only get seven days. It's best if you plead guilty and accept your C.O.'s punishment. I hope she doesn't post you. Here's hoping that you won't get caught, but if you do that you will get off lightly.

All my love darling,
Len xxxx

Joan wanted to say goodbye to her brother who was being sent overseas. As she had already had two home visits for the embarkation of two other brothers, this request was refused. She went home anyway. When she went back to camp she was in trouble but was not put on heavy duties because she was pregnant.

* * *

Margate
2nd April 1945

My Dearest Joan,
I left camp about 12.30 and landed at Manston at 13.30. We had a cup of tea and a bit to eat and then caught a bus to Margate. I was indoors by 14.30. Not bad going, eh! Well dear, you're wanting to know what reception I got. Mum and Dad had quite a shock at first but they are both very pleased about it. Mum is already thinking about getting wool to make things. I called in twice to see your Mum and Gladys yesterday. Wallis was there. They are all feeling very well and Gladys is very proud of her shop. Your Mum also had a shock over the coming Nip, but is O.K. now and looking forward to seeing you.

Keep smiling my love, and take care of yourself. You mean the world to
>Your loving husband,
>Len xxxx
>P.S. I love you lots and lots.

* * *

South Cerney
17th April 1945

My Darling,
Arrived back safely. Apart from that I've no news, just a happy memory. Oh darling I did love my day off this week. We were so happy together in spite of me being a devil at times!!! We seem to belong to each other much

more now. Maybe it's the Nip. Maybe it's just a natural longing for each other and a closer understanding. It makes me happy and want to say "I love my wife" and mean it earnestly with every breath of my life - and I do love you Kid – oh so much. I just want to eat you all up sometimes.

If you as an expectant mother apply for sheets can we later apply for more for setting up house? If so by all means get cracking my sweet. This seems reasonable because I imagine one needs quite a few sheets when having a bambino. I was talking to a chap who said his wife (ex-WAAF) got 150 clothing coupons just by asking for the amount she thought she needed. Apparently she asked for two coats, three dresses, two sets of underclothes and two pairs of shoes.

Pay Parade tomorrow – and another fiver goes into the Post Office. I put £10 away on Monday – didn't feel safe carrying all that money around. I hope the postman delivers this letter to No 7 and not 13. Remember there are two Mrs Manwarings in Kent Road.

Your very own
Len xxx

Joan was discharged on 19th April 1945 after two years in the service on "compassionate grounds" since she was pregnant. The official statement lists her as a wireless operator with the rank of Leading Aircraftwoman and says "her trade qualifications have been satisfactory and her character and general conduct very good."

Joan in WAAF uniform

Joan and Len on wall

Joan on wall at Kent Road

Joan sitting on her bunk wearing regulation WAAF pyjamas, drawn by one of her roommates.

Len and Joan's wedding

Chapter Five

Peacetime

"Kiss for bundle..."
August 1945 – June 1946

THE war ended and Victory in Europe (VE) Day was 8th May 1945. Len was stationed in Gloucestershire and Norfolk until his demob in 1946. Joan was in Margate where I was born in October 1945.

South Cerney
10th August 1945

Hullo Kid,
I didn't get back from the M.O. till 10 o'clock, having waited almost an hour, and then found I was landed with the job of duty instructor and this will be my daily task until I fly again, probably on Monday. I have a cod

liver oil dressing on my arm now. Wasn't quite sure whether to drink it or put it on my arm. Of course the dressing had stuck and when I suggested they took it off quickly I got a smack on my knuckles from the Medical Orderly. She said that method was old fashioned and did a great deal of harm. So I soaked it off much to my relief.

Being back in camp makes me realise what a lovely time we had this leave. Thank you, Darling. I suppose you've seen the news in the papers about V.J. Day leave for the forces. We cannot have our two days off until two days after V.J. Day – when all the civilians are back to work, having eaten everything. Not that I mind really, but after all we want to be with our families just as much as anyone else.

Regards to Henry. I hope he has a nice leave. Hope Gladys is better and is being sensible about seeing the doctor. My love to all at home.

    Your loving
    Len xxxx

Victory in Japan (V.J.) Day was celebrated on 15 August 1945 in Britain, and marked the real end to the Second World War.

* * *

South Cerney
18th August 1945

Hullo Darling,

Don't despair too much because Dave has promised to fly me home next Saturday. So all being well we'll make whoopee for four days then. How did your V.J. holiday go off. We had two days rest here and I must confess I really did enjoy myself but I did so miss my favourite partner. We went to a dance in the camp, ate some very nice cakes and watched a firework display at the control tower. The next evening I saw an ENSA play and it was very good. Now it's back to work again – or back to duty instructor for me.

    All my love,
    Len xxxx

* * *

South Cerney
1st September 1945

Hullo Darling,

It was wonderful to have your letter so soon after my return to camp. I felt we were close together. I did some night flying last night and this morning was going to take a fellow to Mona-Anglesey but the weather clamped on – was I glad! Had a letter from Met – he is at Leuchars – Tommy's old station. He is coming on leave this week so I may see something of him.

6th Sept. Sorry for the delay to finishing this letter. Today I flew one of the instructors down to Portsmouth and another to Holmsley South. On Monday I collected an F/S from Shrewsbury. I'm turning into a little ferry service all by myself. We are definitely working harder now than when the war was on.

Yesterday afternoon I went down town and it proved rather profitable. Here's a list of things I obtained:
>3 bottles of light oak stain
>2 bottles of Dettol
>Enough glass for 14 postcard size picture frames for sixpence
>A pair of slippers, providing my wife sends me 5 coupons

I intend making a clothes horse for you by Christmas – also an ironing board.

I heard Brahms Violin Concerto the other evening in the mess. It was wonderfully refreshing.

Goodnight Kid. I love you always.

Len xxxx

For several years after the war many things were in short supply and people followed the instruction "Make do and mend". I can remember my Mum turning and reattaching collars and cuffs to my Dad's shirts. She also cut bedsheets lengthways and sewed the outsides, which were less threadbare, together which meant there was an uncomfortable seam down the middle. My Dad purchased the appropriate tools and leather so he could repair our shoes. Clothes were rarely new, but were hand-made or hand-me-downs.

*　*　*

South Cerney
30th September 1945

Hullo My Love (and little love),
On Saturday to thrill the public I'm flying in formation with some of the boys. Apparently any one of the visitors may speak to us over the R/T and give us instructions. I bet the R/T procedure will be wizard.

Re the clothes horse. Would you like it sprayed pale green, or just left plain. Do you want it with two arms or three? I'm returning the Utility Furniture application form. Don't we need a kitchen cabinet – and do we need a kitchen table? Decide and fill in please. Also I don't think it advisable to mention the standard lamp – not regarded as furniture.

I went to the flicks in camp last night to see "Arsenic and Old Lace". It's the funniest film I've seen for ages. You really must see it Kid if you can. I've got my medal ribbon now. I'm sending you a piece of it so that you can show the Nip – this is what Daddy got in the war – joke! Writing "Daddy" seemed rather strange – I don't feel at all like one, but I guess you feel very much like a mother.

How are you Kid? This seems to be my constant thought now. The Nip is getting very near. How I wish I could help you my Darling, but I guess this is one of those times when I have to remain useless and you have to take the burden on yourself. I want you to know that I'm with you the only way I can be – in thought.

    Goodnight Kid. I love you
    Len xxxx   x – Nip

Kid was another nickname for Joan. I was called Nip and Bundle, but I was named Gaye Melodie Anne after my Mum's wartime friends.

* * *

South Cerney
6th October 1945

Hullo My Love (and little love?),
Thank you for your letter. I'm glad everything's going along alright. It's getting very close now. Be brave, my Darling, as I know you will. I only wish I could do something. It's not fair that you should have to bear all the pain and trouble. I'm not being morbid but I've been worrying about this for ages. I wish I could suffer the physical pain for you. Pray God it's over quickly.

    The coming of the Nip will be another opportunity to see you. I may not be able to fly home because there's going to be a clampdown on ferry trips shortly, but you know Joan that I'll be with you as soon as I can.

I did my two hours of night flying on Wednesday. Thought I'd get it over early this month. Had a wizard night flying supper – roast beef, sprouts and roast potatoes. I went to the pictures on Friday and saw "A Tree Grows in Brooklyn". One of the finest films I've ever seen, sad yet so very true to life. The acting is superb. I also got a glass cutter the other day – these are almost unobtainable but I got one for 1/1.

Goodnight Kid.
I love you always,
Len xxxx

* * *

South Cerney
8 October 1945

JOAN MANWARING 7 KENT ROAD MARGATE

I AM WITH YOU KID ALL MY LOVE. LEN

This telegram was sent a few days before my birth at my grandmother's home in Margate.

* * *

South Cerney
16th October 1945

Hullo Darling,
Arrived back safely. It won't be long now till I'm home on leave for about 10 days. In the meantime you must rest all you can and eat a little more each day. I'm proud of you Kid – you're very brave. Now we will gradually forget the pain and unpleasant part and look forward to a happy future.

Maybe the doctor has to give you the birth certificate. When you get it could you register it to me here as the RAF documents will want to see it. Goodnight Kid. God Bless you. I love you always.

  Len xxxx xx for Gaye

I was born on 15 October 1945 weighing 4lbs 3 oz. My Dad got a telegram announcing my safe arrival and he was able to get a flight to Manston the next day to see my Mum and to meet me. Every year on my birthday my Dad gave my Mum a bunch of flowers.

* * *

Many relatives sent Welcome Baby cards after my birth and there were several with the following pre-printed message and a suggestion about adding a monetary gift.

Dear Gaye,

You've come into a funny world. A lot of folk are fighting hard to make it a better one, so you can look forward to a happy and worthy life.

There is someone to care for you now. But one day you will be grown-up and have to look after yourself. And then you will find that true success in life doesn't only depend on what those who love you have saved up to give you a good start. It will depend too on whether you have learned to add your own mite.

So here's a small beginning. May it grow and grow until the time comes for you to face the world. Then you will be glad to know that you have something worthwhile to help you on your way – something to which you can feel proud that you too have contributed.

 Health and Love attend you always,
 FROM Auntie Nell

You can attach 6d., 2/6 and 5/- Savings Stamps to this card; they can be used to make a deposit in your Savings Bank Account (Post Office or Trustee); or to buy a Savings Certificate (15/- issue or £1 issue) or a Bond.

* * *

South Cerney
12th November 1945

My Own Darling,

I've a little more news and it's a bit more definite. "A" Flights disbanded this afternoon and tomorrow I go on to Night Flight. I should be there until the station closes.

It's quite a good thing to be on nights. We fly from Blakehill Farm, which of course is a decent aerodrome with runways, and we finish by midnight and come back by bus.

Tomorrow morning I hope to go down town and get the wood for the chairs. I miss you dearest. Those last two days of my leave were Heaven. Did you feel that too, Darling. Thank you Kid. Now I'm hoping and praying for you to get well and strong and get that little sparkle in your eyes. Good to know Gaye has gained so much. She's really doing fine.

Au revoir,
>Your loving Len xxxx
>xx for Gaye if she's good.
>x for Gaye if she's naughty.

* * *

South Cerney
29th November 1945

My Own Darling,
I do hope you are a little better. I'm thinking of you all the time. Ken is back and he and myself and another instructor are going to Little Rissington this afternoon for about a month and then coming back here. Christmas leave is rather a muddle. Apparently the railways are on-

ly allowing 10% of the services – sorry it's now been altered to 1½% - almost negligible.

I have sent off three parcels today. The vanishing cream and cold cream is for you, Darling. Could you look after the sweets and cigarettes for me till Christmas. The tinsel is for your Mum. This posting has been rather sudden and I'm in a bit of a whirl at the moment. Two other parcels are on their way. They contain Pyrex dishes. One casserole and one pudding basin is for us Kid. The other casserole is for my Mum for Xmas but will you keep it till I come home.

Have now arrived at Little Rissington. I've just returned from tea and of course I feel much better now. You know I always improve with something in the old tummy. I'm glad Ken came with me. It would have been pretty deadly by myself as the other fellow is a bit of a twig – for want of a better word. Just before I left Cerney I had your letter. Thank you, Darling. Oh how I love you. It just comes over me in great big waves. I miss you so much and I miss the Nip too. She's such a nice little thing.

Love to Gaye and the family and all my love to you.

Your Len xxxx

* * *

No 2 Mess
RAF Station

Little Rissington
Bourton-on-the-water
Glos
30th November 1945

Hullo Darling,

I seem even farther away from you here. This is rather a difficult place to get out of and the long weekends are now over until I get back to Cerney. Strangely enough my first impressions of this station are rather good. Ken and I went to the flicks in camp last night. They also have a music circle and a Y.M.C.A. – most handy for the odd cup of char. Tonight after tea I had a game of snooker.

No more "gen" about Christmas but I'm still hoping to do it legally. It's O.K. with me to spend Christmas Day in your Mum's place and Boxing Day at mine. Any luck with the Christmas tree yet? There are some nice ones growing in the camp. Shall I ...? At Cheltenham I got an electric fire and four surprises for you. Oh Kid this is going to be a wonderful Christmas. I must get home.

I wonder if you could get me some chewing gum Joan and send it to me. I realise it will mean giving up part of your own ration so if you like we could swap – chewing gum for some of the chocolate I sent home. I've made a list of things to make for you in our home. Priority seems to be to finish one fireside chair, a box or pantry for food and a coal box – and a radio for you. After that I must make a china cabinet (so that I can have my bookcase back of course!).

Au revoir. I love you so much. Love to Gaye Melodie Anne.

Len xxxx

I remember the joy when sweets came off ration in 1953. My friends and I delighted in trips to the local sweet shop and spent ages deciding what to buy. You could get a fruit flavoured chew for a farthing – or five for a penny. Gob-stoppers were a penny each and you kept taking them out of your mouth to see the changes in colour. Sherbet fountains had black liquorice straws so you could suck up the sweet lemony sherbet which made you cough when it hit the back of your throat.

* * *

Little Rissington
Glos.
18th December 1945

Joan Darling,
I'm afraid I'm rather weary and a little fed up – we are still here. I phoned Cerney and asked if our leave had been fixed up and I was told we all had five days off but were not allowed to travel by rail.

Tonight I got my Christmas rations of extra sweets: 4 bars of milk chocolate, some Palm toffee and some butterscotch. I managed to get some port wine. It's only a little – about 1/3 of a pint. Hardly enough to go round in a crowd, but I thought we could reinstate our midnight feasts – and what better time to start than Christmas. Keep your fingers crossed that I'll be home for Christmas.

All my love,
Len xxxx

Some items were scarce for a long time. I was told that a baby was allowed one banana a week, even when I was too young to eat it. Apparently one banana was sliced into pieces and shared by the whole family.

* * *

South Cerney
1st January 1946

HAPPY NEW YEAR

Hullo Darling,
Arrived back quite safely in time for tea. I hope you managed to go to the clinic today and trust you're feeling not too worn out. I hope Gaye will soon settle down because then we can get started on you dear and get you

back to normal. Thanks Kid for such a lovely Christmas. We'll have lots of happy times in the future.

Travelling back I thought about the fire in the front room (OUR front room). Would it be a good idea to have it swept before we clean the room. Mum has a long-handled chimney brush which I can use. I was working things out: with luck we could scrub the front room first – 1½ hours (½ for break), bedroom next – 1 hour (lunch time). In the afternoon we could lay the lino in the front room and move the furniture in during the evening. The next day we could spend leisurely unpacking our various boxes and cases and the next day I could make your coal box and finish your little cupboard.

Well Darling I must away now. Take care of yourself. Good night Kid and Kidlet.

>   Your
>   Loving
>   Len xxxx

* * *

> South Cerney
> 13th January 1946

Beloved,
I arrived back safely. I'm glad you came to the station with me Kid. I'm not as cheesed as I thought I would be.

I'm so full of your love, Darling, my mind thinks it's still at home with you.

We were able to buy oranges in the mess today. I got six and if I can get a box will send some home for <u>yourself</u>. The orange are lovely. I'm eating one now. I keep putting my pen down, having a nibble and then on with the letter again.

Last night I thought out a plan for our holiday, and I want you to give me your views. I think we could do it for under £50.

> **Day 1** Margate to London – possibly an early show
> **Day 2** London to Exeter – lunch on train
> **Day 3** Wander round Exeter, shopping and sight seeing
> **Day 4** Exeter to Minehead (Lorna Doone country) Very cold so you will need your hot water bottle
> **Day 5** Minehead by boat to Cardiff
> **Day 6** Cardiff to Wells
> **Day 7** Travel to London.

I had a wizard sleep last night and woke at 7.45 – too late, I thought, for breakfast. However I thought maybe I'd get a cup of char. Imagine my surprise when I saw grapefruit plus sugar, and as I was about to go to my seat one of the cooks handed me a fried egg and bacon. Well – after they'd brought me round... Boy what a breakfast

– and on top of that there was porridge and cornflakes and very nice milk. Who'd be a civilian!

Most of today I've been over in the Arts and Crafts making bits and pieces. Next time I come home I'm going to be rather loaded as I have something for everyone.

Goodnight Kid,
Len xxxx
Kiss Gaye for me. She's lovely isn't she – but not always, eh, Kid!

* * *

South Cerney
29th January 1946

Hullo Darling,

Thanks for writing. I'm glad you enjoyed your birthday weekend. Had quite a nice chocolate ration this week. Fry's sandwich and half a bar of coffee filled block. But of course you don't like either of those. Terry said he'd only got one handkerchief to his name and couldn't get any more down this way. I said I thought I could get some in Margate so he gave me three coupons. Could you spare the time to get them Kid please – nice big ones and send them to me. I'll give you the money when I come home.

On Saturday someone came round the flight and took quite a lot of stuff. I lost two pairs of flying gloves and that long blue scarf. The C.I.D. are now on the job, but it's practically hopeless.

There is a place down town – two rooms, use of bathroom and kitchen and completely furnished even down to spoons and towels. Downstairs the sitting-cum-dining room has a settee and two easy chairs quite nice but the table is nothing much. The bedroom upstairs has a wizard dressing table – one that you can sit under with a triple mirror. The cost is £1 per week. Almost incredible, isn't it. The fellow who is living there now is being demobbed.

No more news for now my love. I love you so very much.

>You very own
>Len xxxx

* * *

South Cerney
2nd March 1946

My Own Darling,
I'm just resting after having an enormous tea – two helpings of toasted kidneys and tons of bread and butter and jam. How are you Kid? It's so long now since I saw you. I keep saying to myself only another ten days, only another nine, and now it's only a week. But even so it still

seems such a long time to wait, and I know you must be feeling the same.

I trust you're taking your tonic. I only know a little of all you endured and all I want is for you to get well. I hope when I'm on leave you'll be able to have a little rest. I've been thinking of you these last few nights and wondering how you ever survived the cold. Have you still got two feet or are they both frozen off.

Longing to see you on Saturday.

    Goodnight Kid,

    Your very own

    Len who loves you xxxx

This is for G.M.A. x.

P.S. Do you want any superfatted cold cream soap?

* * *

                       South Cerney
                       5th March 1946

Dearest Joan,

Today I've been terribly busy – two trips this morning and another this afternoon together with bags of talking and paperwork. I'm just about on my knees.

I'm counting the days now till our next weekend. Last weekend was a glimpse of heaven. It couldn't have been more perfect. If ever you needed to find the way to my heart you've certainly done so now. Your cooking was wonderful, Darling. I feel an awful pig eating all that pudding. I did enjoy the few hours we had together, Kid. It was wonderful waking in our own home together. I'm happy when I'm with you, Sweetheart. Gaye's a lovely little thing, isn't she? Though I do wish she'd be quieter at night for your sake.

I've been at Arts and Crafts and quite enjoying myself. I've finished the lamp standard for Mum and also the reading lamp for Betty with the exception of polishing it. If you see any nice material for the chairs don't forget to snap it up, providing the coupon value is reduced.

Goodnight Kid – Beloved,
    Your very own Len who loves you. xxxx
    This is for G.M. A. x

Dad spent a lot of time doing woodwork, making small items such as photo frames and mirrors as well as substantial pieces of furniture. I still have several pieces.

* * *

South Cerney
26th March 1946

Hullo Darling,
I hope Gaye has been good and that you've had some good night's rest. Don't forget to go and see Dr Simpson as soon as he is back. Could you please get some late po-

tatoes – King Edwards, I think, are the best. 7lbs will be sufficient, and then put them on pieces of cardboard under the bed in the little room. When I come home next I will plant them.

South Cerney is moving – lock, stock and barrel – to Feltwell. This is in Norfolk, miles from anywhere. Nearest town I think will be Norwich – about 30 miles away. We are due to have finished here completely by April 29th. At first I was overwhelmed by this news, but I've sobered up. I don't think it will be too bad. One of the instructors has a motorbike, and as he intends to come down to Ciren each weekend he says he'll give me a lift to the nearest mainline station. In actual distance I'll be 90 miles from you. Might even fly over one day to see you.

We had an apple for tea today – as well as liver. I think we're having egg and bacon tomorrow morning. Why come home?! I'll leave you to answer that. How is Gaye now, and was her illness due to the vaccination? The nice weather has returned again after a day of rain. Just before it rained the grass all over the camp had been cut, so you can probably imagine what a lovely smell there was about the place. Makes one feel it's good to be alive.

No more today so au revoir.

    All my love, Len

    xxxx

P.S. I think I'm flying an Oxford on Sunday. Rather looking forward to it.

* * *

RAF Feltwell
Nr Thetford
Norfolk
25th April 1946

My Own Darling,

Here is a letter from my new home. It's miles from anywhere but I think once the rest of the people have arrived it will be better. The first day it was just like a ghost town. On the way up here the country gradually got flatter and flatter and less interesting. I flew up here and took less than an hour.

Being one of the first arrivals I did pretty well for furniture – chest of drawers, two lockers, table, two chairs and two carpets. Unfortunately there are no basins in the rooms but I guess I will manage, though there aren't many basins in the ablutions. Joan, could you send me a clock or a watch of some kind. I'm absolutely lost not knowing the time. Possibly Dad could lend me one – would you mind asking.

I miss you so much Joan. I'm glad Gaye is alright. I'm longing to see her again. I wonder if she'll recognise me. Has she developed any new antics yet.

Good night Kid,
    Your loving
    Len xxx

*** * ***

Feltwell
25th May 1946

My Own Darling,
This is the weekend and I should be home with you, but we've all been confined to camp and have helped to raise money for St Dunstan's fund for the blind. Actually it's been quite fun with side shows, treasure hunts and auction sales. Last night there was a dance and I had a fairly good time, but really I need my favourite dancing partner.

It looks as though I've had my pyjamas. Thanks for sending them but I've made enquiries here, but they know nothing about them. We can't claim as they weren't registered so that's that.

Only another fortnight Kid and I should be home for good. I miss you so much my darling. If only I could see you for a few hours – but then I would want it to be longer. No more news for now. Take care of yourself.
    All my love,
    Len xxxx
    xxx for Gaye Melodie Anne

P.S. Have sent in my income tax return and should get a rebate of almost £7. Not bad, eh!

* * *

RAF Feltwell
Norfolk
6 June 1946

My Own Darling,
This is probably the last letter I'll write to you before I'm demobbed. The actual day is next Tuesday and I shall be leaving here Thursday, and will arrive home about 11 o'clock Thursday night. Don't wait up, Kid.

I have to return here Monday night and go to London on Tuesday. Happy Days! My Log Book has been returned and I'm assessed as "above average pilot/navigator and BAT instructor". I have to see the C.O. tomorrow for the final interview and then I've got to wait till Thursday for the M.O. Otherwise I'd be home on Wednesday.

No more now, Sweetheart. Longing to see you again. Good night, Kid.

Your loving Len xxxx
xx for Bundle

Len and baby Gaye

Joan, Len and baby Gaye

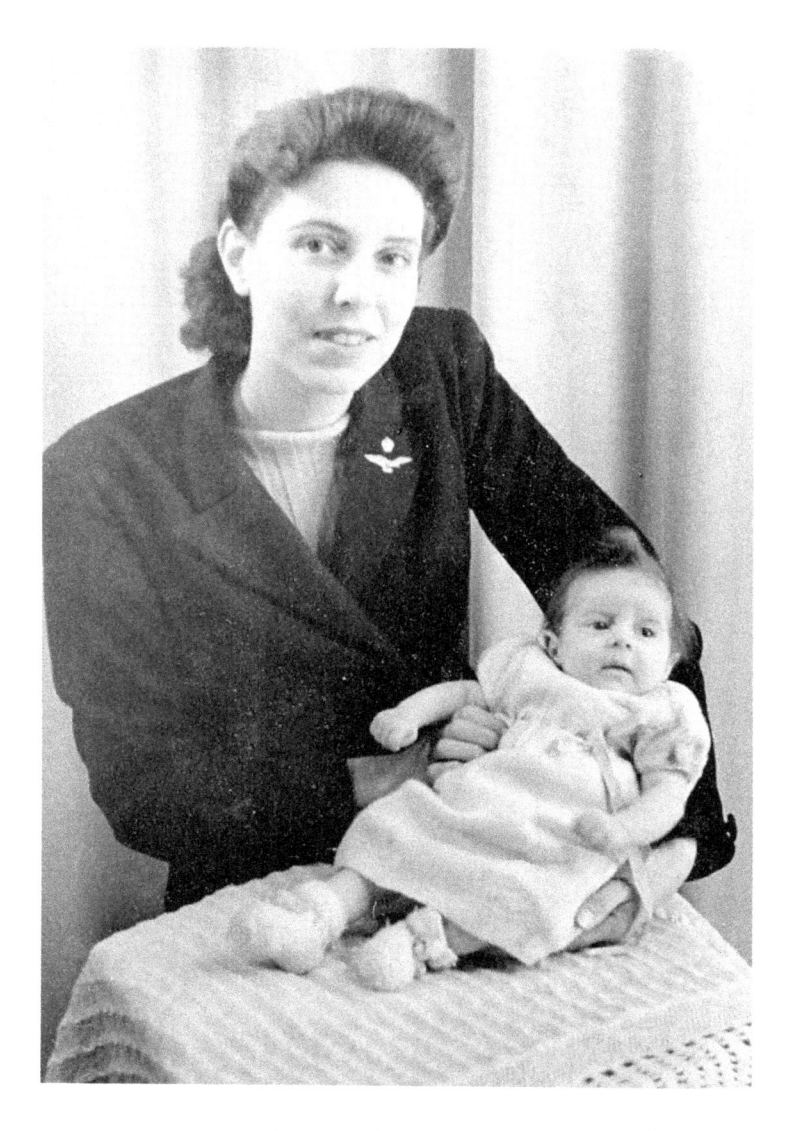

Joan and baby Gaye

Joan and Len, c.1946

After the War

MY Mum and I lived with her mother and sister until my Dad was demobbed. My parents' first home as man and wife was at 14 Kent Road, just opposite the homes of their parents. It was a shared house with a communal bathroom and we lived there until I was three years old.

My Mum's brothers all returned safely from the war, though Uncle George had been a prisoner of war in Germany. Auntie Gladys sadly died when I was only two. I do not remember her, but my Mum said that having to care for me helped her cope with her grief.

My Dad went back into librarianship and was in charge of the reference section at Margate Public Library and so qualified for a council house. We moved into a tired old house in Garlinge, three miles away on the other side of Margate. I loved playing in the garden and my favourite occupation was digging with an old metal poker. One day the poker vanished and I was heartbroken and confused. For years after that when any item went missing, we said "It has gone where the poker went". Much later I discovered that my grandmother had broken her poker and my Dad had given her my gardening tool to replace it. He had not realised I was so attached to it, and so invented this mythical place that housed all manner of missing things. My Dad grew vegetables and kept chickens and rabbits to supplement the limited food available in the shops, since food rationing did not end until 1954.

A couple of years later we moved to a brand new council house in Garlinge. One house on the street had a television, and on Saturday mornings a dozen children would gather there to watch westerns on a tiny black and white set. I went to the same infant and primary school that my Mum had attended, and she got a job as a GPO telephonist working three nights a week. My Dad took his professional exams to become an Associate of the Library Association in 1955.

Money was tight. At weekends we often visited the grandparents. My Mum and I would go by bus and my Dad would cycle there and back. In the summer we sometimes walked there as cross county it was only about two miles, but we got the bus back. I remember a steep farm track and, as we walked down it, my Dad would throw a penny and I would scramble after it as it bounced over the rutted ground. I was once given a florin (two shillings, 24 pence in old money, which is equal to ten pence now) to buy a block of ice cream from the mobile van as a special treat. In my excited haste I dropped the coin in the garden and it vanished. So there was no more money for ice cream, as the florin had gone to where the poker went.

I was spoiled by my grandmothers. My Dad's Nan gave me pink wafer biscuits and ginger marmalade. My Mum's Nan gave me butter balls rolled in sugar and pig's tails. I was fascinated to watch the curly tail straighten out as it cooked before I held it by the end and munched on the gristly meat. I wouldn't want any of them now. But I still enjoy ice cream.

My Dad's Nan always took me to Pritchard's Ice cream Parlour at the top of the high street. The ice cream was homemade, and each scoop contained ice crystals which gave it a crunch. My Mum's Nan took me to Lyons Corner House at the bottom of the high street, and the ice cream was a cylinder wrapped in paper and served in a rectangular dish.

We went to the Festival of Britain in London in 1951 and I went on an escalator for the first time. We stayed with Auntie Dolly in Hayes, Middlesex, and travelled in each day. I loved the London Underground and although at five years old I could read quite well, I misread some of the names of the stations. Black Fairies (for Black Friars) and Charging Cross (for Charing Cross) became part of our family mythology.

Another childhood holiday was a camping weekend with my Dad when I was seven. My Dad fixed a child seat onto his bike and we slept in a tiny tent. We cooked all our meals on a camp fire and explored the countryside. We stayed in a farmer's woodland and his wife gave us some eggs for breakfast.

My Dad then got a job with the Medical Research Council in Harwell in Oxfordshire where he gained his Fellowship of the Librarian Association. We moved to a small flat in Harwell village. After about a year my parents bought a plot of land in Wallingford in Berkshire and my Dad designed a bungalow. It had several unusual features such as a green roof and circular porthole windows in the bathroom and toilet. Small windows on either side of the lounge fireplace were fitted with yellow glass which filled the room with a glow like sunlight.

My Mum worked as a wages clerk at a local agricultural firm and developed her interest in astrology by taking correspondence courses. She gained the gold medal from the Faculty of Astrological Studies for the highest marks in the Diploma exam. She had many regular clients who stayed with her for years. She also became a distance learning tutor for the Faculty. There is an issue of *Open Learning News* which has an article by each of us talking about supporting learners at a distance in our different disciplines.

My Dad continued to work for the Medical Research Council but moved to be in charge of the libraries at the brand new Northwick Park Hospital in Harrow, Middlesex. He retired in the early 1980s and my parents moved to a bungalow in Sussex. My Dad was very active in the local community of Fairlight. He joined the literary society and the gardening club, and became chairman of the village hall committee.

My parents did not talk about the war much but I know their honeymoon was a few days in Reading. On the journey from Margate, their train was tracked by a doodlebug bomb which eventually veered off and exploded in a field. They attended a concert in Reading Town Hall given by the London Philharmonic Orchestra. On their fifteenth wedding anniversary, my Dad recreated the concert they had attended on their honeymoon by purchasing records of all the pieces. My Dad wrote his autobiography about his war by referring to his photographs and his log books, but without reference to the letters which he had obviously forgotten. He also wrote ten novels, and six of them include references to his wartime experiences.

I went to Exeter University and took an honours degree in Zoology. I loved university life, not just the academic aspects but the mix of people, and an introduction to a life-long love of art, music and live theatre. The course was very practical including field trips to Dartmoor, the Scilly Isles and the South of France.

Although I appreciated nature, I was drawn to genetics and cell biology and so I went to Edinburgh for my doctorate in biochemical genetics. I fell in love with Edinburgh and indeed with the whole of Scotland, and the cultural and social life was fantastic. But my research work was disappointing and unfulfilling. It was intellectually challenging but lonely. Like most PhD candidates, I worked as a demonstrator and tutor to first year students to earn some extra money. But I soon found myself caught up in helping them to learn. I ran extra meetings and borrowed biological films and other resources to explain some of the key concepts. These sessions became the highlight of my week, and I realised that a future doing genetics research was not for me.

Professor Waddington, who was head of Genetics, was very interested in education and the department library contained books and journals on biological education. It was there by chance I spotted an advert for a research fellow in biology and education at Glasgow University. I applied and was amazed to get the job – due, I was told, to my enthusiasm. I had only completed two years of my PhD and everyone said if I left then I would never finish it. That was just the spur I needed. I took up the post and moved into a flat in Glasgow. At weekends I returned to Edinburgh to continue with some experimental work and in the evenings I wrote my thesis.

My job at Glasgow was designing learning materials in biology for students to study at their own pace. This individualised learning was based on audio tapes, slides and workbooks, a far cry from the interactive online learning I delivered later in my career. The students took a diagnostic test and we then told them which programmes to study. We set up a room with individual study stations and they booked in. We borrowed an old industrial timeclock from a local shipyard and the students punched in and out with personal timecards. Although the whole scheme was voluntary, they loved the theatre of clocking in and out, but it did make an awful noise.

After six years I moved to Dundee and became a Senior Lecturer at Dundee College of Education, which later merged with the University of Dundee. I developed courses in educational technology offered by distance learning. My secretary, Thelma, was the wife of my Head of Department and I was invited to their home for dinner where I met Andy, Thelma's son. He was a mechanic who repaired my car when it developed engine trouble. We began dating, keeping it quiet until we were sure it would last.

I married Andy Wilson in 1983 in the College chapel. I was delighted that my husband and my parents got on so well. In particular the bond between Andy and my Dad was very strong. We enjoyed several joint holidays. We took a cruise together on the Canberra on our first anniversary and their Ruby Wedding. Andy and I organised a Golden Wedding party for my parents in Sussex in 1994.

I was amazed to be awarded the MBE in 1984 for services to education. I was invited to Buckingham Palace for the investiture. I am sure the regulations are different now, but I was told that the guest list was very strict. The recipient could invite a spouse and two children (but not step children), or a spouse and one parent, or two parents. There was no amount of pleading that would let me invite my spouse and both parents. Of course I invited Andy but I made my parents decide which of them should attend. In the end my Dad came and my Mum waited at home, but her absence was a slight dampener on the whole occasion. Andy and I attended three garden parties at Holyrood Palace over the next few years and enjoyed wonderful food. But there were no refreshments at the investiture ceremony, so I deliberately drank some water from a carafe in the waiting room.

My Mum had many health problems and the last ten years of her life were very hard. She suffered from severe arthritis, emphysema, tuberculosis, a heart condition and had several mini strokes. My Dad was her carer and he became an excellent cook, making cakes and pastry and jam too. The arthritis was unremitting and caused excruciating pain and disability. My Dad pushed her around in her wheelchair, although she did say she sometimes felt a bit like a battering ram as he manoeuvred her through the crowded shops. She remained amazingly cheerful and was always interested in what we were doing, and kept up-to-date with the news in the papers and on TV. Her arthritis made it hard for my Mum to go to the hairdresser, so she was delighted when she met Elizabeth who offered a comprehensive home hairdressing service. They became firm friends. Liz is very talented as a singer and artist, and my Dad asked her to design the cover of one of his early books.

When my Mum died in 2002 aged 80, it was a happy release for her. The undertaker asked for a photograph of her so he could prepare her body with the correct hairstyle and so on. The most recent one was on her Disability Badge. At the funeral we waited for the coffin to be carried into the church. As requested, the wreaths from the chief mourners had been placed on the coffin, and right in the middle was the photo in its plastic case. I quickly removed it and only later saw the cruel irony of the wording "Rother District Council: Expiry Date March 2007".

We were not churchgoers as a family, but followed Christian values. I have always loved exploring churches and would sit and give a short prayer when I entered. When my Mum died I was so upset that I stopped going into churches and did not pray if I was in one. I was angry, not at her death, but that she had suffered so much pain for so long, and I blamed God. I maintained this furious distance for five years. The poem that I wrote in 2004 shows my feelings.

The Case for God: A Capital Deity

I don't believe in God.
How can He let such terrible things happen?
OK. So maybe I do believe in Him.
But He's not doing a very good job is He?
I don't think he deserves that capital letter for a start.

Maybe he is a bad leader, ruler, boss.
But is he evil, malicious, cruel?
Is he uncaring, selfish, lazy?
Or is he just weak, inefficient, incompetent?
Is it worse to think of him as bad or as non-existent?

If I have bad students,
Weak or lazy or dishonest,
I give them another chance.
I ask them to improve and try again.
And I provide support to make their success more likely.

Do I give god another chance?
Do I try to love him?
Do I give him back his capital letter as positive reinforcement?
Maybe He will improve.
Maybe so will i.

Then when I visited Eritrea as part of my University teaching, the negativity evaporated. The local people impressed me with their resilience. After 30 years of war, they were so positive and dynamic. There were many faiths, but they were Eritrean first. When I entered the large church in Asmara I felt an overwhelming sense of peace and lightness. I immediately sat in pew and prayed.

My Dad continued to live in their bungalow in Fairlight, and we maintained regular contact by phone and visits. I also keep old letters, and this is a birthday letter from my Dad in 2005:

My Dear Gaye,
Happy Birthday. You have now entered the Bus Pass Era. For me (and Mum too) you have always been special – a fount of knowledge, of love, of dedication, of concern for others. There may have been one or two lapses but we were never aware of them.

This is as good a time as any to look back at what you have achieved. If I recall only a few of your academic achievements, in all modesty, you must be proud. Mum and I are, and we know it hasn't been easy.

Oh, and of course amid all these activities you found time to seek out a wonderful man as a husband to share your life. Mum and I were so pleased when you and Andy were married. We are so glad to know him and thank him for looking after you. Well you look after each other.

Have a lovely "old" birthday and enjoy yourself and from now on you'll get younger by the day.
Love from
Dad (and Mum who I'm sure is around)

A few years after my Mum died, my Dad and Elizabeth began to see each other. He helped out with jobs in her house and they socialised. Andy and I were delighted. One February we visited Sussex and the four of us went to a garden to see the display of snowdrops. It was beautiful but it suddenly started to snow so we hurried back to the car. The tender way that my Dad warmed Elizabeth's feet was so intimate and loving that we realised they were becoming more than friends.

I always sent my parents an anniversary card in July and as the date approached the year after my Mum's death I asked my Dad if he would still like to receive a card. He replied that he would appreciate a letter instead, so every year I sent him one. This is his reply in 2007:

Dear Gaye,
How very kind and thoughtful of your to send me your letter. I too have been in reflective mood. I shall visit Mum's grave on Sunday and take her some flowers from the garden.

In spite of her long illness and even in those years there were happy times. Memories of her are all around and within me. The early years of our life together were a bit of a struggle though fortunately we didn't realise it at the time. The middle years were good and we both shone in reflected glory of all your achievements.

The remaining years had their good times too in a strange sort of way. I remember when I had shingles and really was not with it, for Sunday lunch, Mum managed to cook beans on toast with a tin of pears for sweet. It was the best meal ever! Life goes on. No-one can ever replace Mum.

And of course Elizabeth would never seek to – she was very fond of Mum. We get along very well, share many interests and of course you and Andy have made her feel so welcome and gone out of your way to include her. Thank you.

I hope your new office will be a good place for you to work in. Good luck in all you do. It's not luck really. It's hard work and careful planning. I know quite a few people appreciate all that you do. Keep well, have fun and make sure that Andy doesn't work too hard. Try to have few days off!

All my love,
Dad
xxx

After his death, Liz of course continued to live in the bungalow and she found an old letter from Len from about 2005:

My Dear Elizabeth,
It's Saturday morning at 11 o'clock and already the place seems empty without you. It's cold too and I haven't the energy to do anything too hectic. So I'll make myself a

cup of tea, light the fire and make a list of things to sort out in the house and garden. Lists are easy to make. They require very little effort and if I make a mistake I can just rub it out. I'm a lazy devil really.

I know what I'll do to pass the time. I'll look out the crossword puzzles and choose the easiest one (leaving the more difficult one for you when you return). I shall count the weeks and then the days and finally the hours until we meet again. It's now 11.30 and I've completed the puzzle and only made one mistake. I must think about something for lunch. It's still too cold to go outside. Thank goodness I no longer need to go out to chop the wood or bring in the coal or clear away the ashes. This is my second winter with a gas fire and I'm loving it.

My thoughts are with you and I hope you have a nice trip to wherever you are going – I forget where. You go to so many places. I've had my lunch and a quick nap on the settee which was intended to be for half an hour. One and a half hours later I woke up in time to make another cup of tea. I must have been tired. I wonder why! Thank you for your phone call to tell me you are safely back so now I can relax. I'll write some more tomorrow.

<u>Sunday.</u> Gordon arrived with my paper and stayed for half an hour. Most of his stories I'd already heard. Just as he was getting into a new one Gaye phoned and he departed so I shall have to wait till next week for the remainder. In the evening I watched the Royal Variety Show. Some acts were quite entertaining – most were

boring. How the Queen suffers these things year after year is a wonder and she still manages to smile.

<u>Monday.</u> Breakfast done and cleared away. Oh! The phone has just rung. Who on earth can it be at this early hour. It's an angel. As I made my way down the hall I knew and hoped it would be you. Hello Elizabeth. Lovely to hear your voice – so alive and happy and excited. No one should feel that bright so early in the morning! Thank you so much for phoning – you seemed so close. Of course you are close. Close to my heart and in my thoughts.

Have a lovely, restful, exciting and wonderful holiday. The time you are away will drag. I'll keep busy. I've already cleaned the teaspoons and other utensils. Take care. Have fun.

    Love from

    Len

        x – is for tonight.

        x – is for tomorrow.

        x – is until my next letter arrives.

Liz also found these notes in Len's desk, probably from 2005:

Your entry into my humdrum almost complacent existence has shattered the equanimity that I had gradually built around me. I was alone yet not really lonely. I was content plodding along at my own pace, looking after the house, garden and Leo, doing the shopping, cooking and washing and in a sense making do. Yet I was happy – or I thought I was.

Can you imagine a gentle whirlwind, a benevolent and considerate being, an elegant beautiful person, with a kind and gentle character who I now believe was also just existing in a sort of limbo and needing just the right stimulus to break forth into the beautiful woman that I now perceive and have come to appreciate to know and to love. That being is Elizabeth. Perhaps you know her or maybe you don't recognise her from my inadequate description. Let me assure you she is all of that and much, much more.

I am happy to do things for her, little things, big things and even when apart my thoughts are often of her. I have become alive once more and I know who to thank, and I am glad. I hope, too, that you are happy to experience the love we share. I am no longer alone and I'm certainly not lonely. You fill my waking hours and my dreams. Your needs are my needs, your love, my love.

In the summer of 2006 Andy and I invited my Dad up to Dundee for a holiday. A couple of weeks before he arrived he mentioned on the phone that Liz was envious as she had never been to Scotland. We immediately invited her too. We all had a wonderful time and they became engaged. We went our local pub for a celebratory dinner and told the staff about the news. The manager nipped next door to Tesco and purchased a small "engagement" cake which they gave us after our dessert. Liz had been looking for a new car and found one in Dundee so she bought it and they ditched their return train tickets and drove back to Sussex in style.

The following June we organised their wedding in Dundee in the same chapel where Andy and I had married. It was officiated by the University Chaplain. I was Elizabeth's maid of honour and Andy was my Dad's best man. We had a reception for a few friends in the local yacht club. It was a wonderful day and I know my Mum would have approved. A few days later the newlyweds drove to Newcastle and set sail on a honeymoon cruise. Liz had sold her house so she moved into Dad's bungalow in Sussex.

A month later they had a blessing in St Andrew's Church in Fairlight followed by a reception for family and friends. It too was a lovely occasion. Elizabeth had chosen the buttonholes for us and by chance had picked my Mum's favourite flower – freesias. As we came out of the church for the photos I slipped away to the churchyard and placed my buttonhole on Mum's grave.

Andy and I enjoyed many trips with Dad and Liz both in Scotland and Sussex. I remember one outing to Ashdown Forest. Spring flowers were in full bloom and birds were nesting. After a good ramble through the woods we were ready for a cup of tea. My Dad insisted that instead of the café in the visitor centre we should use the primus in the boot of his car. He had of course packed teabags, water, milk, sugar and biscuits but it took a while to light the stove as it was so windy.

Then one evening ten years after he married Elizabeth my Dad phoned at 7.15 for a regular Friday catch up. He talked about mundane aspects of his life. He had made an appointment at Boots Opticians for new glasses. He and Liz had been shopping and bought some new pots and pans for their new induction cooker. Three hours later he had a massive stroke. Although he lived for many months, that phone call was the last coherent conversation we had, although I did not realise it at the time.

After spending time in two hospitals and a nursing home, Liz eventually got him home to their bungalow in Fairlight. He so wanted to spend his last few weeks in the home he loved with Liz and his cats. Liz did a wonderful job caring for him, and we went down to Sussex as often as we could. Although the stroke caused severe physical and mental problems, my Dad never lost his sense of humour. As I watched the squirrels through his window with him in December I asked him when squirrels hibernated. Quick as a flash he replied "When they've got enough nuts."

My Dad would have loved his funeral. He had planned the service himself but he would not have expected that his coffin would be led into the church by standard-bearing RAF veterans. As he was laid to rest with my Mum I read out the blessing from his wedding to Elizabeth.

Ancient Celtic Blessing

A weaving of the Peace be thine.
Peace around thy soul entwine.
Peace of the Father, flowing free.
Peace of the Son, sitting over thee.
Peace of the Spirit, for thee and me.
Peace of the One, and Peace of the Three.
This day and for evermore.
Amen

Gaye and Andy's wedding with Len and Joan, 1983

Len and Joan's Golden Wedding Anniversary, 1994

Len and Joan, 2002

Len and Elizabeth's wedding with Gaye and Andy, 2007

Acknowledgements

I AM pleased to record my gratitude to so many people who have helped and encouraged me in this venture. My husband (Andy Wilson) not only supported me but also typed up some of the letters. A couple of our motorhome trips saw me dictating letters to Andy as he typed on his laptop and we gazed out over beautiful lochs in the Scottish countryside. Elizabeth Manwaring (my Dad's widow and also my Mum's friend) found the documents in her attic and has been very generous in her involvement.

The staff at the Montrose Air Station Heritage Centre have been very supportive. Nancy Scott digitised the photographs, and Dan Paton provided valuable historical background. Eddie Small, a colleague at the University of Dundee, introduced me to the publisher and gave useful feedback on drafts of the book.

Many friends have persuaded me to continue with the project in particular: Cathie, Gwen, Fiona, Jill, Josie, Lorraine, Lucy, Roddy, Pete and Sal. They assured me that strangers would be interested in the lives of my family.

Julie and Tom Christie of Extremis Publishing have been helpful and encouraging throughout and I am so grateful for the opportunity to publish the letters.

About the Author

DR Gaye Manwaring has recently retired from the University of Dundee where she was a Senior Lecturer in Education. She worked in higher education for fifty years and was awarded the MBE. Her academic interests were educational technology, curriculum development, evaluation, distance learning, mentoring and wellbeing. She is a Fellow of the Higher Education Academy (now Advance HE) and a Fellow of the Royal Society of Arts. She has published 29 chapters and articles, acted as consultant on 6 other publications, created 18 educational packages, as well as numerous learning units and online modules as part of her normal teaching responsibilities.

She took an honours degree in zoology at the University of Exeter followed by a PhD in biochemical genetics at the University of Edinburgh. She had a joint appointment in Zoology and Education at the University of Glasgow, designing self-study audio-visual learning materials for students. Twenty-five instructional packages on biology were published by Longmans.

She moved to Dundee and taught many undergraduate and postgraduate courses, and supervised and examined doctoral students. Initially in the 1970s, Gaye ran the Postgraduate Diploma in Educational Technology for an international audience. Later this developed into a distance learning programme using a variety of media. In the 1980s and 90s Gaye was heavily involved in nationally funded staff development programmes for schoolteachers, social workers, doctors and community dentists. She was joint leader of a five-year project on Staff Development and Appraisal in which a team of thirty tutors designed training materials and delivered them to staff from every school in Scotland. As Director of the Open Learning Service for the Scottish Council for Postgraduate Medical and Dental Education she produced in-service packages that were sent to every general practice in Scotland. She designed training materials using print, audiotape, slides, CD-ROMs, video, websites and virtual learning modules. The topics included professional development, staff appraisal, health education, evaluation methods, teaching and learning, mentoring, Children's Panel, open, distance and work-based learning.

She has worked extensively with international students and her academic career has taken her to Canada, USA, Poland, Eire, The Netherlands, Croatia, Thailand, Malaysia, Australia and Eritrea. She ran staff development courses for lecturers at the Universiti Sains in Penang in Malaysia, and took leave of absence to work for six months at Murdoch University in Australia. She taught for many years on the Teaching Qualification for Further Education Lecturers and on Dundee's courses for new university teachers.

She joined a Continuing Education class on Creative Writing at the University of Dundee (the Nethergate Writers) and contributed short stories to their published anthologies, including one story about a WAAF stationed at Montrose during WW2. She is currently writing an educational autobiography provisionally entitled "Learning My Living" and a novel "Tadpoles and Fireworks". Her voluntary work has included CRUSE bereavement counselling, Victim Support, audio describing theatre performances in Perth and Dundee, and running wellbeing courses for Arthritis Care. During the lockdown she has been delivering online courses on wellbeing for students. In the future she would like to spend more time motorhoming with her husband as well as continuing with voluntary work on wellbeing.

For details of new and forthcoming books from Extremis Publishing, including our podcasts, please visit our official website at:

www.extremispublishing.com

or follow us on social media at:

www.facebook.com/extremispublishing

www.linkedin.com/company/extremis-publishing-ltd-/

CPSIA information can be obtained
at www.ICGtesting.com
Printed in the USA
LVHW080321170421
684638LV00008B/10

9 781999 696276